ASSESSING
ASSESSMENT

COMPETENCE-BASED ASSESSMENT

ASSESSING ASSESSMENT

Series Editor:
Harry Torrance, University of Sussex

The aim of this series is to take a longer term view of current developments in assessment and to interrogate them in terms of research evidence deriving from both theoretical and empirical work. The intention is to provide a basis for testing the rhetoric of current policy and for the development of well-founded practice.

Current titles

ASSESSING
ASSESSMENT

COMPETENCE-BASED ASSESSMENT

Alison Wolf

Open University Press
Buckingham · Philadelphia

Open University Press
Celtic Court
22 Ballmoor
Buckingham
MK18 1XW

and
1900 Frost Road, Suite 101
Bristol, PA 19007, USA

First Published 1995

A catalogue record of this book is available from the British Library

ISBN 0 335 19023 5 (pbk)   0 335 19024 3 (hbk)

Library of Congress Cataloging-in-Publication Data
Wolf, Alison
    Competence-based assessment/Alison Wolf.
        p.   cm. — (Assessing assessment)
    Includes bibliographical references and index.
    ISBN 0–335–19024–3 (hb). — ISBN 0–335–19023–5 (pb)
    1. Vocational education—Great Britain—Evaluation. 2. Vocational
qualifications—Great Britain—Evaluation. 3. Education and state—
Great Britain. 4. Competency based education—Great Britain.
I. Title. II. Series.
LC1047.G7W65   1994
371.11'3'0941—dc20   94–25710
                                                              CIP

Typeset by Colset Pte Ltd, Singapore
Printed in Great Britain by St Edmundsbury Press Ltd,
Bury St Edmunds, Suffolk

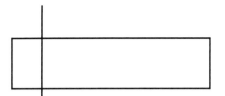

CONTENTS

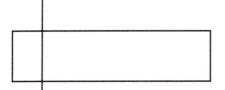

SERIES EDITOR'S INTRODUCTION

Changing theories and methods of assessment have been the focus of significant attention for some years now, not only in the United Kingdom, but also in many other western industrial countries and many developing countries. Critics of contemporary education and training systems argue that real change will not take place in schools and colleges if traditional examinations remain unchanged to exert a constraining influence on how teachers and students approach new curricula or other forms of learning opportunities. Similarly, examiners have been concerned to develop more valid and 'authentic' ways of assessing the changes which have been introduced into schools and colleges over recent years – more practical work, oral work, problem solving, work simulation and so forth. In turn psychologists and sociologists have become concerned with the impact of assessment on learning and motivation, and how that impact can be developed more positively. This has led to a myriad of developments in the field of assessment, often involving an increasing role for the teacher in school or college-based assessment, as more relevant and challenging tasks are devised by examination agencies for administration by teachers *in situ*, and as the role and status of more routine teacher assessment of coursework, practical work, assignments and so forth has become enhanced.

However, educationists have not been the only ones to focus much more closely on the inter-relation of curriculum, pedagogy and assessment. Governments around the world, but particularly in the United Kingdom, have also begun to take a close interest in the ways in which assessment can influence and even control teaching, and in the changes in curriculum and teaching which could be brought about by changes in assessment. This interest has not been wholly coherent. Government intervention in the UK school curriculum in particular has sometimes initiated, sometimes reinforced the move towards a more practical and vocationally oriented curriculum and thus the move towards more practical, school-based assessment. But government has also been concerned with issues of accountability and with what it sees as the maintenance of traditional academic standards through the use of externally set tests.

It is precisely because of this complexity and confusion that the present series of books on assessment has been developed. Many claims are being made with respect to the efficacy of new approaches to assessment which require careful review and investigation. Likewise many changes are being required by government intervention which may lead to hurried and poorly understood developments being implemented. The aim of this series is to take a longer term view of the changes which are occurring, to move beyond the immediate problems of implementation and to interrogate the claims and the changes in terms of broader research evidence which derives from both theoretical and empirical work. In reviewing the field in this way the intention of the series is thus to highlight relevant research evidence, identify key factors and principles which should underpin the developments taking place, and provide teachers and administrators with a basis for informed decision-making which takes the educational issues seriously and goes beyond simply accommodating the latest policy imperative.

Alison Wolf's contribution to the series is a particularly welcome and important one. The book reviews changes in assessment in further education and vocational training, focusing on the claims and problems of a competence-based approach, particularly as exemplified by the development of National Vocational Qualifications (NVQs) in the UK. Wolf has worked in the field for many years, often on Employment Department-sponsored studies, and brings a wealth of theoretical understanding and empirical data to the task of evaluating competence-based assessment. Like many working in applied policy-oriented research, Wolf's work, while well known to 'insiders', perhaps has not reached as wide an audience as it deserves because of the exigencies of moving on to the next problem, the next contract, leaving photocopied research reports to inform policy but not the wider debate. In this extremely well-informed and incisive account, Wolf draws on her experience to review the strengths and weaknesses of a competence-based approach and identify what its prospects might be in the future.

The book reviews the origins of competence-based assessment and looks in detail at the critique of traditional educational systems which is at the heart of a competence-based (and particularly an outcomes-based) approach to vocational training and assessment. Wolf is broadly sympathetic to the critique, agreeing that knowing what, or knowing why, is by no means the same as knowing how, let alone actually being able to translate that knowledge and understanding into competent practice. But she is doubtful about competence-based training and assessment being able to realize its more ambitious claims in practice (an irony indeed). Wolf's doubts derive not only from empirical evidence about implementation problems but also from inherent problems in the model, which she relates to wider debates about the role of criterion-referenced assessment in education more generally. She concludes by suggesting that competence-based assessment has probably reached its 'high-water mark of activity and enthusiasm' and by identifying some areas (particularly in the professions) where it might yet be developed further, but others where it will probably decline.

One of the problems of current debates about assessment, certainly in the UK, is that they have become so polarized and this is especially the case with respect to competence-based assessment. In public at least, it seems one is either a true-believer or a reactionary, self-interested member of the 'educational establishment'; an advocate of work-based assessment or an advocate of paper-and-pencil tests. In private, much more informed and thoughtful debate is starting to take place, largely focusing on the issues and the evidence that Wolf has reviewed in this book. A more open and properly informed public debate is long overdue and *Competence-based Assessment* provides an extremely timely and significant contribution to that debate.

Harry Torrance

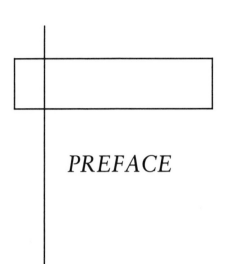

PREFACE

Ten years ago, 'competence-based' assessment, to most people who had heard of it at all, was a rather obscure approach associated with reform movements in American teacher education. Today, it occupies a central place in British education and training, and is the subject of large-scale government support. Competence-based qualifications are considered the major tool in securing 'the Government's aims of increased participation and higher attainment in further and higher education, and hence an improved skills base'; they have 'a key role to play in building a world-class workforce' (HMSO 1993).

Similar views, and similar levels of government support, characterize Australian vocational education and training. A series of Commonwealth reports (notably those of Finn and the Mayer Committee) endorsed competency-based models as a way of better aligning the needs of industry and the outcomes of post-compulsory education, and of reskilling the Australian workforce (Curtain and Hayton 1994). The National Training Board has responsibility for establishing the 'Australian Standards Framework' and competency standards, and these will form the basis of a competency-based Australian Vocational Certificate system.

The concept of 'competences' is also used increasingly in European discussions of vocational training. It appears in the context of a continent-wide debate about the future of education and training. Western countries are conscious that they operate in an increasingly competitive economic environment, characterized by rapid technological change and the disappearance of traditional unskilled jobs. All of them, albeit to varying degrees, feel the need to review and change their traditional approaches to education and training. The idea of competence seems to offer a conceptual framework within which to rethink both content and delivery.

Finally, the idea is being revisited by the Americans themselves. A key component of the Clinton administration's education and training policy is to develop national standards for school pupils' learning, and also 'establish a National Skills Standards Board to promote the development and adoption of occupational standards to ensure that American workers are among the best trained in the world' (US Departments of Education and Labor 1993). The aims and the means, as this book will discuss, epitomize 'competence-based assessment'.

Although the growing interest in competency-based approaches can be traced to worldwide economic and labour market change, this book has a far more specific focus. It looks in detail at how competence-based assessment has developed, with particular attention to the English system of National Vocational Qualifications (NVQs). This focus in turn reflects the author's own experience and the fact that NVQs are currently the most numerous and the most 'mature' competency-based awards in existence. It is also a response to the tendency of their advocates *and* their critics to treat NVQs and competence-based awards as synonymous – to argue that the way NVQs operate is the way competence-based approaches are bound to be. This book asks whether this is indeed the case.

The 'NVQ methodology' (*sic*) is discussed at length in the following chapters. Here we would note that, in the 1980s – following a Scottish lead – the UK Government inaugurated a huge programme of 'standards development'. This produced 'standards of competence' in around 200 occupational sectors, each with its associated qualifications. A set of uniform and detailed directives evolved, which controlled both the form of the standards, and the accompanying awards: NVQs or (in Scotland) SVQs (Scottish

Vocational Qualifications). An important feature of the system is that, although NVQs are recognized (accredited) by a national body (the National Council for Vocational Qualifications), the actual process of assessment is carried out by semi-autonomous bodies which predate the national system. 'Awarding bodies' in the vocational area remain technically independent of the state – as do their academic equivalents, the English examination boards.

NVQs are now firmly established as a part of post-compulsory education and training, although we would emphasize that, even at this level, the number of awards is still dwarfed by those given for conventional academic qualifications. Older-style vocational awards are also still important. Even in the most 'craft-based' of the awarding bodies (the City and Guilds of London Institute) NVQs remain a minority of the awards given. Nonetheless, NVQs are now numerous enough, and long-standing enough, for features of the system to be clearly established and open to appraisal.

Chapter 1 traces the origins of competence-based assessment, and the degree to which current approaches share defining characteristics with older examples of the approach. (Readers who do not have a specialist interest in recent English developments may wish to skip pages 15–29, since these focus on specific characteristics of NVQs rather than on the more general characteristics of the competence-based approach.) In Chapter 2, we examine the arguments in favour of competence-based assessment: why people support it so strongly, and how it compares with more conventional assessment approaches in terms of 'fitness for purpose'. It is these more general and philosophical concerns which have provided the underlying support for current large-scale reforms. Although implementation issues may determine the reforms' actual success and short-term prospects, it is the underlying rationale which will affect the longer-term popularity of competence-based systems.

Chapters 3 and 4 address the extent to which competence-based assessment can deliver on the more ambitious promises made in its name. Chapter 3 examines in some detail the theoretical arguments underlying competence-based assessment. It relates these to the claims made for the larger group of criterion-referenced systems to which competence-based assessment belongs, and argues that these systems have not 'solved' or abolished fundamental issues relating to clarity and assessor judgement. The stark contrast between competence-based and other assessment systems, which is drawn by the most devoted proponents of the former, cannot be sustained.

Chapter 4 looks in some detail at relevant research on the implementation of competence-based approaches. Because relatively little evidence is available on competence-based approaches of the contemporary kind, this chapter also draws on studies of minimum competency testing, and on competency-related assessment in the professions outside the NVQ system. The chapter underlines strongly the importance of understanding that assessment is not simply a technical affair, but operates within complex institutions which themselves have a social and economic context. It notes that there have been very many implementation problems associated with NVQs, and argues that these derive ultimately from a failure to recognize or accept economic and organizational constraints. Finally, in Chapter 5, the prospects for competence-based awards are reviewed briefly. Some conclusions are offered regarding what is essential or non-essential, desirable or undesirable, in a competence-based approach.

ACKNOWLEDGEMENTS

This book is the result of my own decade-long involvement in debates about competence-based assessment. This covers much of the time that such debates have dominated training policy and vocational education in the UK. Inevitably, my own ideas have changed considerably in the process. There is a good deal of hindsight in the chapters that follow. I would like to acknowledge this, and emphasize that I was no more omniscient about what could, or could not, be achieved than the civil servants and consultants who actually developed and implemented UK policy. Equally, I would like to thank the many, many people in government service with whom I have discussed and argued about competence-based assessment over the years, and to acknowledge their openness to criticism, and their willingness to fund research which might not give them the answers they wanted. I hope they will find this book not only fair, but useful in pointing out policy options and alternatives for the future. I would also like to thank the training schemes, lead industry bodies, awarding bodies, colleges, employers, teachers and trainees who have been so willing to give their time to research projects and enquiries, and whose help – and friendliness – is greatly appreciated.

When this book was first discussed with Open University Press, it was as a joint venture: a co-authored text involving myself and Harry Black, Depute Director of the Scottish Council for Research in Education. Work and family pressures forced Harry to withdraw, but we talked about the 'next' book in which we would draw together our mutual experiences of assessment at post-16/post-compulsory levels. Harry died suddenly in the summer of 1994, so there will never be that next book. I would like to acknowledge, in particular, his tremendous insight into the realities of designing assessment systems, and his ability to bring together theoretical concepts and practical experience. He was a humorous and delightful companion, as well as the most helpful and constructive of critics, and he will be sorely missed.

Three people in particular have not only read parts of this manuscript, but have contributed greatly to its development. My ideas about the nature of assessment, and assessor judgements, have developed during frequent conversations and discussions with Harvey Goldstein and the results of these permeate this book. Bob Wood's work on 'standards' and on workplace assessment is a source of ideas and insights to which I return constantly, and has, again, affected the whole development of my arguments and conclusions. Aidan Pettitt first encouraged me to develop the propositions about the theoretical underpinning of competence- and criterion-based assessment, which appear in Chapter 3 (and, in rather different and fuller form, in the monograph which Aidan edited for the Further Education Unit (Wolf 1993a)). Long discussions with him were enormously helpful in both tightening and refining my arguments, and clarifying their implications for practice.

The series editor, Harry Torrance, has been an exemplary source of substantive and stylistic suggestions, and of rapid turnaround. Magdalen Meade, my secretary, has been invaluable not only in her management of much of the work this book draws upon, but in finding lost references, checking curious facts, and in taking care of last minute panics.

Authors generally thank their families. I would like to do the same. In the course of finishing this book, I have become even more like Lewis Carroll's White Rabbit than usual, and my husband and children have borne this with remarkably little complaint – and provided a great deal of support. I am not sure if the results are worth it, but I am certainly very lucky to have them around.

THE EMERGENCE OF COMPETENCE-BASED ASSESSMENT

'Competence' and 'competencies' are vexed terms, over whose definitions acres of print continue to be expended. Rather than drag the reader on a tour of these definitions, their advantages and failings, I want to start with a (borrowed) definition of my own:[1]

> Competence-based assessment is a form of assessment that is derived from the specification of a set of outcomes; that so clearly states both the outcomes – general and specific – that assessors, students and interested third parties can all make reasonably objective judgments with respect to student achievement or nonachievement of these outcomes; and that certifies student progress on the basis of demonstrated achievement of these outcomes. Assessments are not tied to time served in formal educational settings.

This definition has two major strengths. First, it encapsulates most of the key features of competence-based assessment as it is actually being developed and promoted at present: most especially in vocational, technical and professional education and training in the UK. Second, it is originally an American definition and signals the American origins of much of the debate. Competence-based assessment, and competence-based education, are, in their most widely practised and preached forms, essentially American ideas. The philosophy of competence-based assessment, as discussed in the 1980s and 1990s by, notably, the British and the Australians, is packed with direct echoes of US literature of ten years before. What is dramatically different are the institutional structures which characterize the United States on the one hand, and the UK and Australia on the other; and which have produced very different patterns of implementation and growth in competency-based programmes.

The three components of competence-based assessment which are especially important, and which the definition above encapsulates are:

1 The emphasis on outcomes – specifically, multiple outcomes, each distinctive and separately considered.
2 The belief that these can and should be specified to the point where they are clear and 'transparent' – that assessors, assessees and 'third parties' should be able to understand what is being assessed, and what should be achieved.
3 The decoupling of assessment from particular institutions or learning programmes.

These characteristics define the practice of competence-based assessment. For example, in England, which has gone furthest towards embracing competence-based assessment as a national policy, its foremost proponent has entitled his book *Outcomes* (Jessup 1991). However, the emphasis on outcomes and 'transparency' is not peculiar to the competence-based context. It is also a defining characteristic of a rather broader church, that of *criterion-referenced assessment*.

Criterion-referencing is a more familiar term to most people than competence-based assessment, having been advocated within education since the early 1960s. Its advocates put forward many of the arguments which we meet in the competence-based literature, for example about the need to move away from norm-referencing and ranking to an emphasis on what students can actually do, and about the beneficial effects of clear criteria on teaching and learning (see Glaser 1963; Popham 1978). Indeed, in England, the early arguments in favour of what was to become a fully-fledged competence-based system refer explicitly to a 'criterion-referenced' approach (Jessup 1991: 167).

The detailed methods adopted by criterion-referenced and competence-based assessment also make it clear that the latter is a specialized development of the former. Criterion-referencing, too, is concerned with clearly specified outcomes, and with assessments that address these outcomes separately rather than dealing with 'pass marks' or 'norms'. It is built around the minute specification of these outcomes: a 'domain descriptor' which is intended to be so clear and unambiguous that reliable, parallel assessments can be derived from it directly. And while criterion-referenced tests can, in principle, involve 'cut-offs' at various levels, they have come to be associated primarily with single passing scores and with the concept of testing for mastery, just as competence-based assessments have done.

Criterion-referenced assessment has been a very influential approach in recent years, notably in the design of the English National Curriculum which was introduced in the late 1980s. The new curriculum was produced in the form of supposedly clear and free-standing descriptors of what pupils at different 'levels' should attain, with these levels supposedly independent of the pupils' age and school class: a pure application of the basic theory of criterion-referencing. (For discussions and critiques see Brown 1988; Noss *et al.* 1989; Torrance 1994.)

Criterion-referencing, too, hails conceptually from the United States. Nonetheless, competence-based and criterion-referenced assessment are not synonymous. The latter is generally associated with mainstream education, with the criteria defined by the school curriculum, and with paper-and-pencil tests. The former, by contrast, involves an idea of competence which is essentially non-academic. In practice, as noted by the same American text from which our first definition was derived,

> It tends ... to derive from an analysis of a prospective or actual role in modern society and ... attempts to certify student progress on the basis of demonstrated performance in some or all aspects of that role.
>
> (Grant *et al.* 1979: 6)

In other words, it is vocational in the broadest sense, and bound up with the idea of 'real-life' performance. Indeed, in its early days in the United States, 'performance-based' assessment (and education) were the terms used more often than 'competence' (Tuxworth 1989).

In this book we will be discussing, for the most part, competence-based assessment in this more specific sense; i. e. assessment of a 'competence' which relates to an occupational role. However, at relevant points, we will also be referring more generally to the characteristics it shares with criterion-referenced assessment in general – and to evidence from occasions when attempts have been made to identify and implement 'competency testing' in non-vocational settings.

The origins of modern competency-based assessment: US reform movements

Competency-based assessment (in association with competency-based education) first became important in the context of American teacher education and certification. It was associated with growing concern about the state of American schools and educational standards; with attacks on the quality of teacher education (and recruits into teaching) which received wide publicity (see especially Conant 1963; Koerner 1963); and with demands for greater accountability.

One response to this concern was a new involvement by federal government in education reform. Education in the United States is essentially a state and local concern. A separate Education Office at federal level was established only in the 1970s. Federal funding remains a tiny percentage of education expenditure. Nonetheless, it has been extremely important in launching various reform programmes and developments intended to act as levers on education nationwide.

In the 1960s and early 1970s, one of the areas to which federal policymakers responded was the call for greater accountability.[2] There was considerable enthusiasm for highly specific objectives and learning plans in a variety of contexts. (This was also a period when researchers talked enthusiastically about Computer Assisted Learning that would produce 'teacher-proof' materials and lessons.) Teacher education was under quite general attack, as undemanding and irrelevant to the classroom, and as one major cause of the malaise in American education. 'Performance-based' or 'competency-based' teacher education was seen as a major and promising reform possibility: something whereby 'the collegiate programs could radically be improved . . . [with] a chance to truly make a difference in the preparation of teachers and in the education of children' (Andrews 1972: 4).

The catalyst was to be government funding. It was a combination of federal funding and state legislatures' determination to tighten up and improve teacher certification requirements that drove the movement forward.[3] In Chapter 4 we will be reviewing what has happened to competency-based teacher education in the United States in the ensuing years. Here, we would emphasize the importance of the grants which the United States Office of Education provided to a number of teacher education institutions to develop model training programmes for teachers. These involved the precise specification of competences or behaviours to be learned, all of which must, by implication, be acquired by a teacher before certification. The American Association of Colleges for Teacher Education – again with federal funding – undertook a major publishing and dissemination exercise on the associated ideas (though without ever formally endorsing the model). A number of states moved to requiring competency-based certification programmes for teachers.

The literature published in the early 1970s highlights the features of competency-based assessment which we have already identified in brief, along with other, crucial implications for how the system should operate. It involves: 'precise objectives stated in behavioral terms'; 'explicit and public' criteria for actual assessment; and a rejection both of set times for learning, and being assessed, and of entrance requirements for candidates. Only the 'exit requirements' associated with competence displayed should matter. At the same time, intensive 'needs assessment' was seen as essential to identify where candidates were already competent, and where they might need additional learning/teaching; and also as a precondition for personalized programmes and for individualized assessment.

The same model was apparent when 'competence-based' reforms were introduced to other areas of United States further and higher education. Once again, the agent of reform was an activist federal government agency, and, once again, the arena was formal higher education institutions. This time, the impetus and funding came from the Fund for the Improvement of Postsecondary Education (FIPSE), an autonomous unit within the huge Department of Health, Education, and Welfare, which encouraged colleges and universities to develop competence-based curricula and assessment approaches in a variety of occupations, providing development grants for that purpose. Here, too, there was some concern for greater efficiency, and discontent with the accountability and quality of teaching institutions. More important, though, was a reformist rejection of the notion that 'formal course work should remain the only pathway to a credential, and . . . doubt that traditional course content bears much relation to the future performance of many students' (Grant *et al.* 1979: 10). The competence enthusiasts of FIPSE were concerned, above all, with enhancing opportunities and quality for the new students whom huge expansions in higher education (and increasing demand for skills and credentials) had brought into the system. What is striking, however, is the reform focus of the competency movement: how far removed it was from reflecting some broad social consensus, and its limited long-term impact on higher education. Even at its height, very few institutions were directly involved: and even in those that were, interest and awareness was generally confined to the 'experimental' programme receiving federal funding (Riesman 1979).

If we look from 1970s' America to the competency-based assessment of 1990s' Britain, what is striking are the huge similarities between the model developed by American reformers, and that promulgated by British enthusiasts. There are differences in the consistency and speed with which competency-based recommendations have been translated into compulsory national assessment programmes. The differences are institutional, but the motivating forces are remarkably alike.

Competency-based assessment appealed to reformers of both the right and the left at a time when the UK Conservative Government had become convinced of the need for major reforms in the vocational and training sector. Huge increases in youth unemployment in the late 1970s and early 1980s had created an emergency response in the form of work experience programmes, for which longer-term and more structured objectives were needed. At the same time, there was growing national consensus emerging that future prosperity was threatened by our failure to educate and train enough of our young people and our existing workforce.

Almost any other industrial country was seen as superior to the UK in this respect. For example, the report on 'Competence and Competition' published by two government quangos[4] compared the UK unfavourably with systems as disparate as the United States, Germany and Japan. While there have been a few dissenting voices (for example, Shackleton 1992), the basic diagnosis has become even more generally accepted, across the political spectrum, in the last few years. Vocational training is seen as both a national imperative and an area of current failure.

No reform movement would be adopted as government policy, however, unless it was congruent with UK Conservative Government philosophy. This has generally combined a belief in 'market' solutions and the wisdom of business executives with a profound distrust of any bodies mediating between it and the individual, whether they be directly elected (like local education authorities) or quasi-corporate (like the professional associations). The first important Government proposals were contained in a White Paper of 1981, the 'New Training Initiative', one of whose major objectives was to reform apprenticeship (and reduce union power) by abolishing time-serving and tying qualifications directly to the individual's demonstrated attainment. The objective was to

> develop skill training including apprenticeship in such a way as to enable young people entering at different ages and with different educational attainments to acquire agreed standards of skill appropriate to the jobs available and to provide them with a basis for progression through further learning.
>
> (Manpower Services Commission 1981)

A reference in the same White Paper to this involving 'standards of a new kind' provided the basis for a huge programme of 'standards development' carried out by the Manpower Services Commission, discussed further below. It also signalled the influence of reformers who saw competency-based standards and assessment as the way forward. They did not consider themselves to be natural allies of a right-wing government in other respects. Their concern was to open up access, especially for 'non-traditional learners', and their dislike was not for unions but for educational establishments which they felt to be overly academic, self-interested, élitist, and a bar to equal opportunity.

For them, too, competency-based assessment was beguiling

because it cut out all intermediate institutions. Gilbert Jessup, the most prominent English advocate of competency-based testing, and the Deputy Director of the National Council for Vocational Qualifications, argues that we have had 'a provider-led system', in which the learner is frequently neglected. He claims:

> The measure of success for any education and training system should be what people actually learn from it, and how effectively. Just common sense you might think, yet this is a comparatively new idea.
>
> (Jessup 1991: 3)

Competency-based assessment, in the reformers' view, created a system in which the learner or candidate *was* central. With direct access to the 'standards' of competence, people could see exactly what was required and put themselves forward for assessment without interference.

Although the ideas underlying English competency-based assessment were originally formulated in the United States, their influence on English policy was greatly increased by their prior adoption in Scotland. The Scots, during the 1980s, carried out a major reform of their secondary education system, including introduction of the 'National Certificate', which brought all non-advanced vocational education under a single rubric. The National Certificate embraces large numbers of modules, which can be separately delivered, or combined into qualifications. They are offered in schools or colleges and are developed and accredited by the Scottish Council for Vocational Education (SCOTVEC). They are based on criterion-referenced or competency-based outcome statements.

At the same time, the modules remain essentially educational in purpose, designed for young people in full-time schooling, and many of them are relatively traditional in their overt concern with mathematics, language skills, etc. While the English system drew on the Scottish experience for ideas and for individuals with experience in introducing the National Certificate, its ambitions were more far-reaching and self-consciously opposed to the 'educational establishment'.

This too struck chords with the Conservative Government which believed that standards in education had fallen dramatically, and that this was in large part the fault of teachers who embraced egalitarian ideas dating from the 1960s. In mainstream primary and secondary education, this belief inspired a programme for large-scale testing of children's attainments within the new National Curriculum. The idea was to use direct measures of this type to compare schools' 'outcomes', bypass obstructive intermediaries, and increase accountability and attainment. The competency-based system they were offered seemed to promise the same results in vocational education and training.

Vocational education and training in England and Wales: the context of competence-based reforms

Before describing in some detail the way that competence-based assessment has been developed into a complete national system in England and Wales, it is worth reviewing the institutional context into which the reforms were introduced. There was, until the introduction of National Vocational Qualifications in the mid-1980s, no formal, overall structure for non-academic education and training post-16. The statutory bodies concerned with industrial training have traditionally fallen within the purview of the Employment Department rather than the Department for Education, and have preserved enormous degrees of autonomy. Their numbers and titles reflect the gradual growth of new occupations and professions, along with their need for qualifications for substantive but also status reasons. Many guard their independence jealously.

This provides a marked contrast with most of Europe, where strong institutional structures, regulated at national level, have responsibility for education and training and carry assessment conventions and accumulated expertise. In France, for example, all national qualifications fall within the preserve of the central ministries, and reforms are carried out within a system where politicians generally accept the legitimacy and professional skills of the education bureaucracy. In Germany, too, although the implementation of vocational training is the concern of local chambers of commerce and individual employers, they work within a highly consensual but also all-encompassing federal structure which lays down training regulations, and authorizes qualifications.

The lack of structure in English vocational education became increasingly apparent as the sector grew. Non-academic education for post-16-year-olds has been the fastest growing sector of English education throughout the post-war period. Most such students are to be found in the 'further education colleges' formerly run by local education authorities, and now independent institutions under a central government agency. In 1994 two-thirds of 16–18-year-olds in education attended these colleges. Most followed vocational courses, but also, increasingly, studied for academic A-levels. Students following vocational courses include full-time students following one- or two-year courses, apprentices, other part-time students on release from employment (e.g. accounting students) and, in increasing numbers, young people who, on leaving school and failing to find employment, enter the Government-funded Youth Training schemes which involve alternation between workplace and 'off-the-job' training.

Further education colleges have always received funds from a number of different sources (including employers). However, as part of the Government's thrust to reorganize and increase the volume of vocational training, funding from the Employment Department, which is earmarked for particular programmes, has become increasingly important. The Employment Department was given resources with which to fund a large part of 'Non-advanced Further Education' in further education colleges on a discretionary basis, with the object of encouraging programmes responsive to industrial needs. In addition, many young people on Youth Training schemes came (and come) to further education colleges for their 'off-the-job' training. While Employment Department funding traditionally was funnelled through regional and local government offices, there have been major changes associated with the introduction of 82 Training and Enterprise Councils (TECs). These largely autonomous bodies, on which local industry is heavily represented, now have responsibility for disbursing programme funds, and for evaluating and responding to training needs in their area.

Compulsory education (to age 16) was conceived as leading to A-levels for an academic élite, and school-leaving for the remainder. Consequently, the examination boards responsible for school exams were never encouraged to develop vocational or technical examinations. Most vocational awards were, and are, offered by independent bodies deriving from craft and professional associations. For example, banking examinations are run by the Chartered Institute of Bankers, accountancy examinations by the chartered accounting bodies. All are very careful of their independence. However, within further education colleges, dealing predominantly with 16–19-year-olds, the 'big three' multi-occupational awarding bodies dominate. Two of the three are notionally quite independent of the state: the City and Guilds of London Institute, which ran most of the assessment and accreditation for craft occupations such as construction and catering, and the Royal Society of Arts which dominates the clerical field.

The third, the Business and Technician Education Council (BTEC), was established by the Government in response to the perceived crisis of the 1970s, namely, a shortage of technicians and highly qualified office staff.[5] While BTEC awards can be taken by students on release from employment, many are taken by full-time students: 16–18-year-olds in further education (studying for First or National Diplomas) and older students in higher education studying for Higher National Diplomas which are a technical, sub-degree level award. While BTEC awards are essentially vocational, they have always contained a relatively large amount of general education, especially in such broad areas as business and finance. They have been increasingly popular with young people looking for a less academically demanding alternative to A-level, which offers chances of progression and which does not overly prescribe a definite vocational choice. While the 1980s showed a general, albeit slow, increase in staying-on rates as a whole, BTEC courses grew considerably faster than more occupationally specific offerings.

What existed up until the 1980s was thus a nascent tripartite system, but one in which only the academic A-levels were a coherent part of the education system, and in which other vocational and technical awards suffered from the complexity of the awarding system, and the almost total lack of understanding, by higher education and employers, of what the different awards meant, and how they might relate to each other. During the 1980s, however, the Government's responses to youth unemployment moved beyond emergency work programmes to a large-scale effort to reform and systematize vocational education. This was spurred on by the accompanying near-collapse of the apprenticeship system (generally examined by City and Guilds) under a combination of recession, structural change in key industries (e.g. the downsizing of the engineering workforce) and the high wages for apprentices which had been secured under successive wage agreements.

The first emergency work-experience programmes for the young unemployed were set up by the Manpower Services Commission, a quasi-independent subsidiary of the Employment Department which has since been abolished, with its functions integrated into that department. These programmes were developed and strengthened over time, so that the current Youth Training programme has clear requirements for training towards a vocational qualification. It has also become compulsory, in effect, for young school-leavers who have neither found employment nor are following another educational or training programme.

Youth Training schemes most resemble the German dual system in structure and philosophy, but deal overwhelmingly with relatively low-status craft awards and office training. They also tend to be seen as a last choice, with none of the prestige associated with proper apprenticeship, or with the more desired options within the German dual system. Considerable amounts of funding are also channelled into Employment Training (ET) or Training for Work for unemployed adults. This, too, is intended to lead to vocational qualifications – and specifically competence-based National Vocational Qualifications (NVQs). However, training courses offered tend to be short and, again, concentrated on lower-level awards.

Training for the young and the long-term unemployed has taken up large amounts of Government funding, and most of the attention of the Employment Department and, more recently, the Training and Enterprise Councils (TECs) who now run Employment Training and Youth Training. These latter programmes are also the main locations for the award of NVQs. However, the Government also saw competence-based awards as playing a central role in upgrading the skills of people in employment. Their vision was of large numbers of employees pursuing vocational awards in the workplace, with hundreds of thousands of workplace supervisors assessing and certifying them. All this would come about because the development of *competence*-based awards would mean that qualifications reflected workplace roles directly and completely, and would uncouple the acquisition and certification of skills from time-serving either at work or in the classroom.

In 1986, the Government's Review of Vocational Qualifications identified a coherent qualification structure as the necessary pre-condition for a training system designed to serve the young and the older worker, the employed and unemployed. It led directly to the creation of the National Council for Vocational Qualifications. This has a remit to establish an NVQ system of approved vocational awards, involving a clear and simple hierarchy (currently of five levels). By this time, 'competence' as a term had entered Government policy. The review argued that 'assessments carried out by many bodies do not adequately test or record the competences required in employment', that 'assessment methods tend to be biased towards the testing either of knowledge or of skill rather than of competence', and that there are 'many barriers to access arising from attendance and entry requirements' (Manpower Services Commission and Department of Education and Science 1986). The education sector, at this stage, was seen as essentially in opposition to needed reforms.[6] Instead, the reformers saw NVQs as the vanguard of a more far-reaching change in training and education, more enabling, less élitist. Government ministers, in turn, were happy with a system which disdained the 'educational establishment' and saw industry representatives as the source of all wisdom on vocational education and training.

Figure 1.1 summarizes the reforms in the nature and structure of vocational qualifications, all of them involving a move away from traditional assessment methods to a completely competence-based approach. Change is being implemented gradually across the whole economy, and is meant eventually to incorporate professional groups as well as craft, manufacturing and service sectors. The system is discussed in more detail in the next section. In essence, the qualifications which use this approach derive from the activities of *industry lead bodies* which represent their industry and are responsible for drawing up detailed standards of occupational competence. These, in turn, are to be used as the basis for vocational awards.

There has been no official change to the status of the awarding bodies, although they have inevitably become closer to government in the process (and, with large amounts of government development money at stake, reluctant to take public issue with any policy). Moreover, in theory, standards are public property, and different bodies may offer awards based on them. In practice, there

Before reform: myriad self-regulating awarding bodies

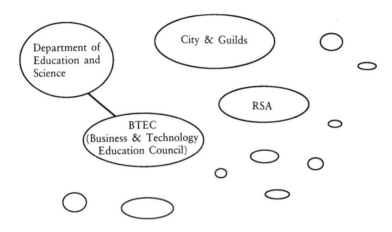

After reform: lead bodies (representing industries) submit standards to NCVQ for approval

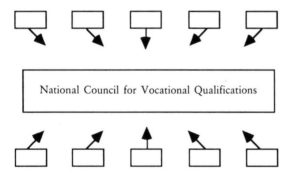

Awarding bodies submit qualifications based on standards to NCVQ for approval

Figure 1.1   Vocational qualifications system in England and Wales, before and after reform.

are considerable tensions in the system, because occupational groups have differing pre-existing relationships with different awarding bodies, and because some lead bodies wish to set up as awarding bodies themselves. What has happened is that the big three vocational awarding bodies have all expanded their activities, and instead of operating in a semi-monopolistic way, with the vocational/prevocational market carved up between them, now compete much more overtly for trade.

A fully fledged competence-based system: National Vocational Qualifications

The basis of the whole system of competence-based awards is the 'standards programme'. Current Government policy requires the Employment Department to develop 'recognised standards of competence relevant to work' which are to be 'established by industry-led organisations, validated nationally and incorporated into vocational qualifications' (Debling 1989: 77). A 1988 White Paper, 'Employment for the 1990s', emphasizes that

> These standards must be identified by employers and they must be nationally recognised. Thus we need a system of employer-led organizations to identify and establish standards and secure recognition of them, sector by sector, or occupational group by occupational group.
>
> (Quoted by Debling 1989)

The employer-led organizations are the 'lead bodies' referred to above, which have been established and funded by the Employment Department and, in principle at least, are fully representative of their industry. In practice, of course, this tends to mean that there is a small group of enthusiastic industry representatives, more or less self-selected, who meet at regular intervals very much like a company's board, but with the backing of a secretariat of some sort. The actual process of developing standards is generally carried out by consultants (funded by the Government) with the lead body providing general oversight.

The 'standards' embody and define competence in the relevant occupational context. However, they have to take a very precise form, following guidance developed, quite early in the process, by a small group of committed civil servants and consultants. Standards must, first, be based on a *functional analysis* of occupational roles. As Fletcher (1991) explains:

- This involves beginning with the *key purposes* of the sectoral occupation and identifying the *key functions* undertaken.
- The concept of functions is highly important. Many earlier analysis techniques focused on tasks, which represent a lower level of activity. The following may be helpful in distinguishing between these different terms:

  Tasks – activities undertaken at work.
  Functions – the purpose of activities undertaken at work.

  (Fletcher 1991: 167–8)

The functional analysis enables the analyst to identify the key outcomes – those related to the underlying purposes. Those key outcomes must then be turned into units and elements of competence, expressed in outcome terms. It is here that criteria appear, in the form of the 'performance criteria' which are at the centre of the standards; 'These reflect the critical aspects of performance – all those qualities which are essential to competent performance' (Fletcher 1991: 169).

Because the format and even the language of standards are so tightly defined, and involve such unfamiliar terminology, only a limited number of people have actually been able to draft them. Thus, a new lead body, in receipt of a governmental contract, would also receive the names of individuals or organizations approved for standards development. These people could then be invited to tender for the development of the new body's own occupational standards. The existence of this rather small group, well known to each other and to the key Government officials, inevitably strengthened the tendency of the development process to generate a private vocabulary and conventions which were opaque or incomprehensible to outsiders. Ability to use the right language came to seem more important than knowledge of the sector – although at least one major lead body responded by hiring occupational experts to draft the standards, and then a special 'terminology consultant' to translate these into the proper vocabulary.

Standards and qualifications

Although 'standards' can, in principle, be used in a variety of ways, in practice Government funding has been directed largely towards their use for National Vocational Qualifications. The Government intends NVQs, eventually, to encompass all the vocational awards which students wish to take or employers to recognize. No qualification will be recognized as an NVQ unless it is based on the standards issued by the lead industry body concerned.

The National Council for Vocational Qualifications approves awards as NVQs, based on this and other requirements encompassing, for example, provision for quality maintenance and access. The process of NVQ accreditation does not involve any formal discussion of curriculum (except insofar as it is implicit in the standards) or approval of learning programmes. The assumption is that use of the standards will ensure the latter's quality. It is part of NCVQ policy that awards should not be tied to course attendance or 'time serving'.

Because NVQs are the most prominent, large-scale current attempt to use 'competence-based assessment' it is worth examining in some detail what they actually involve and how the basic principles of a competence-based approach are carried through not just at institutional level (as in the United States experiments) but as part of a national qualification system.

The formal definition of a National Vocational Qualification is that it is 'a statement of competence' which incorporates specified standards in 'the ability to perform in a range of work-related activities, the skills, knowledge and understanding which underpin such performance in employment' (Training Agency 1988/9). Thus, while NVQs are, in a general sense, criterion-based assessments, they are also not just primarily but *essentially* vocational qualifications. As we have seen in describing the lead bodies' structure, and like the American examples with which we began, they derive their models of competent behaviour from analyses of actual (or, occasionally, prospective) workplace roles.

As national qualifications, NVQs are also based on the fundamental assumption that, for each industry, there exists a single identifiable model of what 'competent' performance entails. The idea that, for each role, there exists such an agreed notion of competence, which can be elicited and will command consensus, is fundamental to any assessment system of this type. It is also, as we shall be discussing later, an extremely ambitious, and a suspect, assumption.

Each NVQ covers a particular area of work, at a specific level of achievement and fits into the NVQ framework of five levels. (Levels 1 to 4 are clearly defined, with Level 5 covering anything beyond. The upper levels of the framework have been under discussion with the 250 UK professional bodies and with higher education for some time, but further elaboration of the framework is unlikely in the near future.) The level of an NVQ is associated not with years of study (as in, say, the French system), but with the nature of the associated work role. Thus Level 1 refers to 'competence in the performance of work activities which are in the main routine and predictable', and Level 3 to 'competence in skilled areas that involve performance of a broad range of work activities, including many that are complex and non-routine'.

In the early stages of NVQ development, it was expected that the level of an award would be determined solely by scrutiny of the 'real' content and applicability of a role, regardless of historical status and the educational background of entrants. In practice, this has proved impossible and unacceptable. NVQ levels generally correspond to the levels of any comparable pre-existing awards: while the Government has also introduced direct equivalencies with academic awards. For example, Level 3 corresponds notionally to A-levels, i. e. to the level of the English academic examinations taken at the end of secondary and beginning of higher education.

NVQs are based directly and totally on the standards developed by lead bodies. Standards are not simply one of the elements being fed into qualification development – to all intents and purposes they *are* the qualifications. The original governmental directive, which required that new qualifications be *based* on standards, would, in fact, have been quite compatible with a more syncretic approach. However, the view of assessment held by the system's creators (and discussed in detail in Chapter 3) led them to reject any further developments (such as the addition of syllabuses) as both unnecessary and, in fact, at odds with the philosophy of accrediting competence however acquired.

The structure of an NVQ is illustrated in Figure 1.2, which demonstrates their modular or unit-based structure. These units consist of groups of 'elements of competence' and their associated

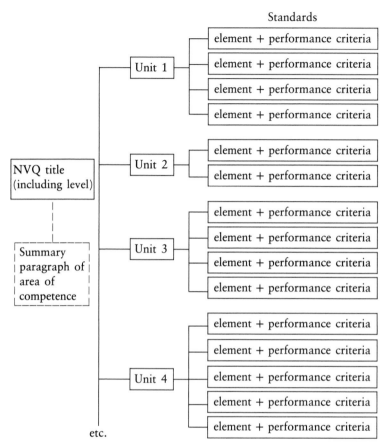

Figure 1.2 The structure of a National Vocational Qualification.

performance criteria, and the idea is that each should reflect a discrete activity or sub-area of competence: a 'discrete function carried out by an individual within an occupational area' (Fletcher 1991: 243). Rather more prosaically, they are seen as the smallest unit worthy of separate accreditation – much like an academic module in fact (NCVQ 1991: 12).

An element of competence is a description of something which a person who works in a given occupational area should be able to do. It encompasses some action, behaviour or outcome which has real meaning in the occupational sector to which it relates. Sample element titles are:

- create, maintain and enhance effective working relationships (management competences);
- inform customers about products and services on request (financial services competences).

The issue of being outcome-based is of prime importance. While competence-based systems vary in their interpretation of what outcomes may be, in NVQs what counts as an outcome is very tightly constrained. The examples above are legitimate because they involve an *active verb* and an *object* – i.e. they are performance-based – and because they are not tied in any way to particular training programmes. Elements of competence which deal directly with processes – for example, with developing fault-finding skills as opposed to showing that one has found faults – are, by contrast, rejected as insufficiently concerned with the final competence, as are any elements which are about knowing and understanding underlying theories. Basic skills such as mathematics and communication can appear only in the context of the performance, not as separately listed or assessed concerns.

In this, NVQs take the competence-based philosophy to its logical conclusion. Other competency-based assessment systems have been considerably less restrictive in the sorts of modules and evidence they accept. For example, an exposition of the ideal type of competency-based teacher education in the United States describes a training programme and assessment system in which separate courses on educational psychology continue to figure:

> [The] field of study . . . [is] broken down into a number of segments of knowledge about child psychology. For example, the teacher should know what range of behaviors at any given age level are considered abnormal and why. That's a skill that can be analyzed on the basis of cognitive performance, in other words how well you're able to answer questions concerning this on a test.
>
> (Andrews 1972: 3)

An example like this makes clear the status of competency-based assessment as a particular variant on the more general 'criterion-referenced' category. However, it would be viewed by the architects of the NVQ system as dangerously far-removed from the performance philosophy which competency-based systems embrace.

Performance criteria

Competence-based assessment is made concrete through highly specified performance criteria. These are the statements by which an assessor judges whether the evidence provided by an individual is sufficient to demonstrate competent performance. Advocates of the approach also emphasize their potential contribution to effective training and learning. Fletcher, for example, argues that 'Competence-based standards are available to assessors and assessees. Individuals know exactly what they are aiming to achieve and assessors can provide specific feedback' (Fletcher 1991: 66).

Performance criteria have a strictly controlled form in the NVQ system, although in some manifestation they are common to all competence-based approaches. Thus, for NVQs, they must consist of 'a short sentence with two components – a critical outcome and an evaluative statement (how the activity has resulted in the required result)' (Fletcher 1991: 66). In effect, the performance criteria state explicit measures of outcomes. Table 1.1 provides an example of an element of competence with its performance criteria. Assessment requires that the candidate demonstrate successfully that he or she has met *every one* of these criteria.

Competence-based assessment for NVQs

The requirements for competence-based assessment in the NVQ system may be summarized as follows:

1 *One-to-one correspondence with outcome-based standards.* This must be comprehensive: evidence must be collected to show that a candidate has met every single performance criterion. Failure to do this, it is argued, removes an essential characteristic of the system – the fact that we know exactly what someone who has been assessed can do (or at least has once been able to do).
2 *Individualized assessment.* Candidates should be able to present themselves for assessment on relevant criteria and elements as and when they are ready to do so, and the necessary assessment and recording systems set up to allow such 'assessment on demand'.

An important aspect of ensuring that individuals have access to assessment is provision of *accreditation of prior learning* (APL) facilities. The NCVQ guide notes that 'APL gives

Table 1.1   Sample performance criteria from an NVQ element. Financial Services (Building Societies) – Level 2. Element title: 'Set up new customer accounts.' Provided as an exemplar in *The Guide to National Vocational Qualifications* (NCVQ 1991)

- Internal/external documents are complete, accurate and legible, and delivered to the next stage in the process to schedule
- All signatures/authorisations are obtained to schedule and actioned promptly
- Correspondence to customer is accurate and complete, all necessary documents enclosed, and despatched promptly
- Correspondence to other branches of society and other organizations/professional agencies is accurate and complete, all necessary documents enclosed, and despatched promptly
- Cash transactions and financial documents are processed correctly and treated confidentially
- Computer inputs/outputs are accurate and complete
- On completing the setting up, the account is filed in the correct location
- Indicators of contingencies/problems are referred to an appropriate authority

---

candidates credit for existing competence. It means candidates need not undertake further training in areas where they are already competent and encourages them to attempt further learning and assessment. . . NCVQ requires awarding bodies to provide APL' (NCVQ 1991: 25). The emphasis on APL reflects the reforming origins of the competence-based movement – in England as in the United States – and its desire to open up qualifications to new sorts of candidate. A large amount of development funding has been put into APL and in Chapter 4 we shall be reviewing some of the evidence on its success.

3 *Competent/not yet competent judgements only.* Only two judgements can be made: either the person has consistently demonstrated workplace performance which meets the specified standards or they are not yet able to do so – 'competent' or 'not yet competent'. Grading is rejected – the idea being that someone either has or has not reached the level required by a holistic model of competence. How individuals perform in comparison to others is irrelevant.

4 *Assessment in the workplace.* NVQ guidance specified that: 'Performance must be demonstrated and assessed under con-

ditions as close as possible to those under which it would normally be practised.' In the early days of NVQ development,
NCVQ was insistent that very large proportions of assessment
must take place through direct assessment in the workplace,
mistrusting the reality (or 'validity') of other forms of assessment. Jessup argues that:

> assessment of performance in the course of normal work
> offers the most natural form of evidence of competence and
> has several advantages, both technical and economic.
>
> (Jessup 1991: 51)

Shirley Fletcher agrees: 'Assessment on an ongoing basis uses
normal workplace performance as its basis, and this continuous
assessment process helps in the identification of training
needs' (Fletcher 1991: 66). However, implementation difficulties
(discussed in Chapter 4) and a commitment to maintaining
access to qualifications (and increasing the numbers of NVQs
awarded!) have modified the position considerably. While it is
still accepted that an NVQ must contain at least some
direct 'performance evidence', increasing amounts of simulation
and so-called 'supplementary questioning' are accepted.

5 *No specified time for completion of assessment.*
6 *No specified course of learning/study.* The only condition for
  achieving an NVQ is successful assessment on all performance
  criteria.

Conditions 5 and 6 reflect the insistence, noted previously, on
separating qualifications from any notion of time-serving, and on
making them available to anyone, whatever their educational or
employment background.

The next logical conclusion is, of course, that the best people to
assess are workplace supervisors or first-line managers – people
who have first-hand and regular contact with the individuals who
are being assessed. In Chapter 4 we examine how far this has
actually proved practicable.

*The quest for clarity: range statements, knowledge
specifications and assessment requirements*

The above section has outlined the basic structure of NVQs and
shown how they have developed the general characteristics of

Table 1.2 'Help children to recognise and deal with their feelings':
Element from Childcare and Education NVQ Level 2

Performance criteria

4.3.1 Children are encouraged to express their feelings in words and
actions and through play in the safety of a secure and accepting
environment.

4.3.2 Methods and activities used to explore feelings are appropriate
to children's level of development and enable them to begin to
recognise, name and deal with their own and others' feelings in
socially acceptable ways.

4.3.3 Emotional outbursts and negative reactions from children are
dealt with in a calm and reassuring manner whilst ensuring the
safety of the child concerned and minimising the disruption to
other children.

4.3.4 Learning opportunities that arise in the daily routine are used to
help children develop their understanding of feelings and social
relationships.

4.3.5 Opportunities to help children extend their vocabulary of words
relating to feelings are developed where possible.

4.3.6 Any concern over the recognition and expression of feelings in
individual children is shared with parents, colleagues or other
professionals as appropriate to the situation.

4.3.7 Ways of expressing and dealing with feelings are demonstrated
by the candidate in appropriate situations.

---

competence-based assessment into a list of prescriptions without
modifying in any significant way the definition with which this
chapter began. Throughout, the emphasis has been on the clarity
which this approach promises to both assessor and learner, and on
the benefits this offers in terms of effective learning, access and
opportunity, and an education and training sector oriented to the
needs of users not 'producers'.

However, the short history of NVQs has also been one in which
the quest for clarity has produced an ever more complex and complicated 'methodology'. As with all competence-based systems, the
assumption has always been that assessment will be unproblematic
because it simply involves comparing behaviour with the transparent 'benchmark' of the performance criteria. Unfortunately, in
practice this turns out not to be the case. In later chapters, we will

Table 1.3 'Obtain and evaluate information to aid decision making': Element from Occupational Standards for Managers

---

Performance criteria

(a) Information requirements are identified accurately and re-evaluated at suitable intervals
(b) Information is sought on all relevant factors affecting current or potential operations
(c) Information is relevant and is collected in time to be of use
(d) A variety of sources of information are regularly reviewed for usefulness, reliability and cost
(e) Opportunities are taken to establish and maintain contacts with those who may provide useful information
(f) Methods of obtaining information are periodically evaluated and improved where necessary
(g) When normal information routes are blocked, alternative methods are tried
(h) Information is organised into a suitable form to aid decision-making
(i) Conclusions drawn from relevant information are based on reasoned argument and appropriate evidence

---

be discussing both the technical and the empirical reasons for this. Here we simply illustrate it by a couple of examples. Those in Tables 1.2 and 1.3 are drawn from (respectively) an NVQ at Level 2 and one at Level 4 + . The first is intended to apply to a playgroup assistant or registered childminder; the other to a manager obtaining an MBA. *Yet the first could equally well apply to a teacher, a paediatric nurse or a child psychologist, the second to a porter at an office reception desk.*

Readers who are interested in the minutiae of NVQ methodology are referred to the official guidance. The important point here is that, before many NVQs had been assessed, this lack of clarity had become noticeable to those concerned. Their first step was to institute a new notion, that of the 'range statement'. These statements quickly became a compulsory addition to all standards (including those previously approved by NCVQ and forming the basis of NVQs already offered in training schemes, workplaces and colleges). Range statements officially 'elaborate the statement of competence by making explicit the contexts to which the elements and performance criteria apply. Also they put limits on the specification to ensure a consistent interpretation' (NCVQ 1991: 14).

In other words, by contextualizing the performance criteria, they hopefully make clear whether it is a psychiatrist or a childminder we are discussing. However, in other respects they have remained extremely nebulous. As a recent survey indicated (Mitchell and Wolf 1992) they have become something of a rag-bag, containing any sort of information for which there is no other obvious home in the standards, and which the latter's authors think might make things clearer. They do, however, impose further assessment requirements. We noted above that assessment has to cover everything in the standards. This means that competence must also be assessed 'across the range', and evidence provided of the candidate's performance with respect to *every* item named in the range statement. This has greatly increased requirements which were already very demanding in terms of time and organization: the consequences are discussed in Chapter 4.

Range statements were rapidly followed by another compulsory addition to standards: specifications of underpinning knowledge and understanding. A common concern of all competence-based reforms is to counteract what is seen as a 'knowledge bias' within testing procedures, especially when the latter are administered by educational institutions. It has also been assumed that knowledge requirements are legitimate only when clearly required in, and for, performance. However, as we noted above in describing American examples, competence-based approaches elsewhere have frequently specified knowledge separately. In the early days of NVQ development, there was considerable disagreement on this issue. However, in the end those who opposed separate specifications of knowledge prevailed. Standards (and NVQs) do not have separate elements or units dealing with knowledge or theory, but instead are intended to create performance criteria (and range statements) which make the necessary underpinning knowledge clear and apparent.

This approach proved optimistic. While the reformers drew strength from the complaints of employers whose recruits 'know what to do but have little experience of actually doing it' (Fletcher 1991), NVQs were soon being criticized for the opposite: for producing people who might be able to demonstrate performance but would have no understanding of what they were doing (see for example Prais 1989; Norris 1991). Moreover, consultative work-shops which tried to 'extract' or 'induce' knowledge requirements from standards demonstrated quite quickly that the knowledge extracted was not, in fact, at all standard, but subject to very different interpretations (see Chapter 4). Concerned to fend off a mounting attack on NVQs as narrow and undemanding, NCVQ added separate 'knowledge/understanding' lists to every element of competence.

Finally, the transparency of assessment requirements came into question in its turn. The theory of competence-based assessment, as we saw at the start of this chapter, is that clear definition plus the existence of workplace expertise make assessment unprob-lematic. Assessors may need some training in understanding the nature of particular terminology; thus, in the NVQ system, 'assessor awards' have been developed which take assessors through the meaning of terms, the process of record-keeping, and the like. But the actual process of recognizing, and so assessing, competence in one's own vocational field is seen as unproblematic. Checking that tests are valid and reliable is reduced to a single per-formance criterion in a single element of a lower-level award, so simple is it seen to be within the constraints of a standards-based system. As one exposition puts it:

> For the workplace assessor, operating within a competence-based assessment system, the actual products of performance provide evidence to be matched against specified standards. A workplace assessor will seek evidence of performance which matches the element, performance criteria and range statement for each unit of competence. Where evidence is not available from normal working practice, or would be difficult to generate, the assessor may need to set up supplementary assessments.
>
> For example, a competent worker may be one who is able to deal with a number of contingencies – machine breakdown, sudden changes in workload or priorities, or even a fire. It would obviously not be practicable for an assessor to cause a deliberate breakdown of machinery (or indeed set fire to the building), simply to assess an individual's ability to cope. In this context, therefore, an assessor needs to be skilled in providing opportunities for supplementary

assessment. This may involve a skills test, questioning of the individual, or allocating a new task or job.

(Fletcher 1991: 68)

These tasks will supposedly be carried out by workplace assessors in their thousands and tens of thousands. Once they know the standards, and recognize how they relate to their own workplace, it is assumed that the rest will follow easily: evidence will be accumulated in an individualized way, to suit the requirements of the individual learner, while still maintaining national standards.

In Chapter 4 we will be reviewing the empirical evidence on how far this prediction is actually borne out by workplace experience. Here, we simply note the fact that, just as 'range' and 'knowledge statements' have been added to standards, to plug perceived holes in the dike, so too have assessment requirements. Lead bodies are now expected – from first principles, not through piloting and experimentation – to add lists of 'assessment specifications' to the standards which examining and awarding bodies use. Yet another level of detail and centralization is thus added, and it would be rash to see it as necessarily the last.

NVQs represent a very particular application of competence-based assessment, albeit the largest and most well resourced to date. They are also, as has been indicated, the most tightly defined in their format and application. In the following chapters, we will be looking first at the underlying reasons for the attraction of competence-based approaches and the arguments in favour of such reforms, and second at the degree to which the underlying theories are coherent and sustainable. Third, we look at the evidence on implementation, in England and elsewhere.

Before doing so, it is important to emphasize, once again, that competence-based assessment is essentially vocational in its concerns – albeit vocational in the widest sense. It is from the idea of professional and workplace competence that it obtains its rationale; and in understanding NVQs, in particular, it is important to emphasize that their architects were concerned primarily with workplace accreditation, industrial training and efficiency, and opportunities for the workforce – not with full-time education. Since 1992, education in England has also been introducing 'GNVQs' or 'General National Vocational Qualifications'. These, too, are accredited by NCVQ, but they are not, in spite of their name, competence-based awards in any recognizable sense. They are vocationally oriented but otherwise fully integrated into conventional educational patterns of delivery and assessment. As a text on competence-based assessment, this book is concerned with NVQs and their equivalents elsewhere. GNVQs in their current form will therefore not be a major focus of discussion.

2

THE CASE FOR COMPETENCE-BASED ASSESSMENT

Grand claims are made for competence-based systems, and they also tend to be associated with highly specific approaches and a completely new vocabulary (as outlined in Chapter 1). This, along with their espousal as part of more general political and policy objectives, tends to obscure their original rationale. Chapters 3 and 4 will be largely taken up with problems and unresolved issues associated with competence-based assessment, and it is therefore important to review the arguments in favour of a competence-based approach.

The arguments are essentially to do with the role of education and training as vocational preparation. Of course, there is a sense in which the whole of education has some sort of vocational relevance. However, it is often very indirect, and overlain with important proximate goals such as the development of general critical faculties, the development of aesthetic or artistic skills, or the pursuit of particular branches of academic knowledge. In late twentieth century Britain, the rhetoric of 'competitiveness' and 'relevance' holds sway over the idea of liberal education as championed by Cardinal Newman. The latter argued for the pursuit of knowledge for its own sake, because it satisfies a direct need of human nature even though it be turned to no further account, nor subserve any direct end ... To open the mind, ... to refine it, ... to give it powers over its own faculties is an object as intelligible ... as the pursuit of virtue.

(Newman 1852: 4, 23)

Unfashionable though this view may be, there remain clear differences between courses with a specific vocational purpose, and general education, whether at primary, secondary or higher levels.

Much of the most impassioned opposition to the notion of competency-based education has come from those who see it as part of a 'competency crusade' to take over the whole of higher education (Penington 1992) – a view admittedly encouraged by some of the most enthusiastic proselytizers for the approach (Burke 1989, Jessup 1991). However, the core of competency-based approaches has always been vocational and professional education and training. It is here that the concept of competence can be given a coherent meaning, and operationalized with some real success; and it is here that the arguments for adopting competence-based reforms can be made with force and conviction.

The concept of 'competence' has, not surprisingly, been defined in a whole range of different ways, many of them quite unrelated to the idea of a competence-based assessment system. The most important for our purposes, however, is the one associated with the major reform movements in vocational education instituted in the UK by the then Manpower Services Commission (a semi-independent quango of the Employment Department, since absorbed into it) and by the National Training Board in Australia. The simplest and most accessible way in which these agencies use the notion is to describe competence as 'the ability to perform the activities within an occupation'. Thus 'By competent we mean performing at the standards expected of an employee doing the same job' (Manpower Services Commission 1985). As Wood notes:

This ... definition ... says 'Think of trainee X and imagine substituting him/her for employees Y and/or Z. Would you notice a significant difference in terms of getting the job done?' It is a functional definition of competence; it describes how someone who is judged competent will look.

(Wood *et al.* 1989: 3)

This definition is highly workable at one level – notably within a firm – while creating myriad implementation problems at others. As discussed in detail elsewhere, it seems in practice to encourage narrow mechanistic definitions of what 'performance' involves, even though it should also permit of the broadest of interpretations. It also leaves unresolved the awkward transition from the level of particular workplaces to those of national standards and formal training and education institutions. However, this definition also has two enormous advantages. It underlines the essentially vocational nature of competence-based training and assessment; and it defines the difference between the ideal and the actuality of much existing vocational education.

The competent plumber is the one who can build or mend an efficient central heating system, not the one who can define a substance's specific latent heat of fusion. Doctors deservedly attract patients on the basis of their 'bedside manner' (which can reassure, and thereby elicit information, and aid diagnosis) and not simply their ability to score more than 50% in anatomy examinations. The fact that current competence-based awards are now being criticized so heavily for their neglect of 'knowledge' makes it important to emphasize the well-founded position from which they begin. It is that theoretical knowledge – 'book learning' – stands in very uncertain relationship to practical expertise. The stereotypes of the absent-minded professor and the incomprehensible expert reflect a common reality.

Unfortunately, theoretical knowledge has two enormous advantages from the point of view of those responsible for delivering vocational and professional education. The first is that it is (relatively) easy and cheap to deliver on a large scale and in a standardized way. The second is that it accords with the concerns and status hierarchies of the education industry itself. Together, these two sets of influences exert a constant pressure towards the assessment and certification of expertise on the basis of educational rather than vocational performance. It is this pressure – and its visible results – which competence-based assessment attempts to counteract.

The education industry

In understanding the pressures which shape modern assessment systems, the scale of education is crucial. For an ideal type of competence-based assessment, one need look no further than the medieval guilds, with their system of apprentices, masters and masterpieces. The original 'masterpiece' was not some arcane composition or unique work of art. It was the craft product which demonstrated that a young craftsman had reached a level of expertise at which he might be admitted to a guild as a 'master' – a fully fledged professional. The 'masterpiece' in question might be a piece of goldsmith's work – but it might equally well be a fine pair of shoes, or a blacksmith's wrought weathervane. It displayed applied knowledge – practice, or the German notion of *technik* – at the highest level, and comprised the assessment on which the formal qualification was based.

Trying to translate these sorts of assessment and qualification practices into a modern setting immediately throws up multiple problems. The first is simply the nature of most modern occupations, which do not have the distinctive, highly specific sets of skills which characterize the crafts. We return to this issue in Chapter 4, in describing how a particular competence actually gets defined for assessment purposes. The second is the nature of teaching and learning – itself related to the structure of modern industries and enterprises. Craft training and assessment are based on the one-to-one relationship between master and apprentice, whereas most modern education, including most professional and vocational education, takes place in formal educational establishments, in large groups, with a teaching staff characterized by rapid and regular turnover. This means that things have to be standardized and formalized, in ways which are quite unnecessary when teacher and assessor are one and the same, when the relationship is direct *and long term*, and when the only external reference group that matters is that of other guild members in a small tightly knit community.

There are significant differences between countries in the degree to which all vocational education is the job of formal educational institutions, and in the degree to which apprenticeships remain important. Germany (and Switzerland and Austria) retain something far closer to traditional apprenticeship for all their vocational education than do any other developed countries. Throughout the world there are important elements of apprenticeship in training for the old professions such as law and medicine, and many of the newer ones such as accountancy. However, in all these countries and occupations, there has been a move towards formal, detailed codification of both syllabus and assessment procedures, which operate at national (or occasionally cantonal/state) level. Moreover, in every case – including apprenticeship – important parts of the training process take place in formal classrooms and workshops, away from the workplace.

The situation is partly a reflection of the nature of modern occupations and industries, in which personnel also turn over rapidly, in which travel and changes in job responsibilities are the order of the day, and in which it is very difficult to reconcile major teaching responsibilities with the way people's jobs are structured. But it is also, to a very large extent, a reflection of the way in which a national (and international) labour market has emerged, in which qualifications are used as currency over time and space, and expected to be standardized in a way which was quite irrelevant in the labour market of mediaeval Europe or even the nineteenth century industrialized world.

These qualifications are not only national (or international) in application. There are also far more of them – not only in absolute terms, but relative to the population. In the United States, for example, where around a half of the population now undertakes some form of higher education, there has been a huge growth of university students, from 3.5 million in 1960 to 12 million in 1980. Even more striking, in 1870 there were only 50 000. The population has grown sixfold meantime – the student population over 200-fold. More recently, with a virtually stable population, we find UK student numbers tripling between the early 1960s and the late 1980s – and showing a further 33 per cent increase over the next five years.

As recently as 1950, only 5 per cent of young people in Western Europe completed academic qualifications offering the possibility of university entrance (A-levels/Baccalauréat/Abitur or their equivalents). The French Government aims to have 80 per cent of the age cohort following a baccalauréat course by the year 2000, and in the last five years alone the proportion following such courses has risen by 15 percentage points. In England, almost one-third take A-levels. A further one-third is expected to take 'Advanced' GNVQs which are also formally acceptable for higher education entry. Even in Germany, with its well-established apprenticeship system, Abitur students now outnumber apprentices and certificates have quadrupled in the last 20 years.

In this sort of situation, cost and easy replicability of assessments become a paramount concern, even if it is not the one which is most readily articulated and expressed. And the simplest and most easily replicated assessments are, in fact, written ones – especially those based on simple recall of facts, but also, more generally, those which use brief questions, written scripts and standardized marking schemes. They take fairly little time – for either adjudicators, markers or the examinees themselves, they can be sent around the country easily, they can be rescrutinized if there are queries about results, and they are visibly and demonstrably easy to administer in a 'fair' and equal fashion.

The importance of this last point is difficult to exaggerate. It is almost inevitable that, the more important formal qualifications become, the more they will be expected to concur with the norms of formal fairness and transparency of rules. Wood has emphasized the importance of external assessment in making qualifications credible. The English GCE exam,[7] he notes, won respectability in large part because 'great play was made of the impartiality and fairness to candidates (and teachers)' which external testing guaranteed, and 'because when internal assessment was conceded, care was taken to contain the influence it could have on the final grade' (Wood 1985: 33). Employers, he says, tend to like examinations. Their use by the universities and professions gives them high status, but their apparent fairness and objectivity are quite as important.

An ever-increasing emphasis on explicit rules, formal procedures and 'rational' legitimation for any activity or institution is a defining characteristic of modern societies (Weber 1964; Habermas 1975). Weber's analysis of the historical shift from traditional to 'rational-legal' authority is encapsulated in a small way in the shift from the master–pupil relationship, where expertise, and the right to establish curriculum, assessment and pass-mark were embodied in an individual, to the world of modern assessment systems. Here, syllabus, assessment procedures and marking schemes are ever more explicit and open to scrutiny. (Even old 'school certificate' papers have none of the clarity about mark allocation of a modern GCSE examination.) Formal complaints and appeals procedures are the norm, often because of legislation to that effect. Central governments establish bodies – in England and Wales, NCVQ (the National Council for Vocational Qualifications) and SCAA (Schools Curriculum and Assessment Authority) – to oversee, check and report formally on the fairness and accuracy of assessment methods. The United States has experienced by far the most challenges to the legality of assessment systems and results (see Chapter 4), but students in a number of European countries have also had recourse to the courts over assessment results.[8]

These same factors manifest themselves at the level of assessment methods and individual items. Europeans tend to be extremely critical of the United States' reliance on multiple-choice tests for university selection, and professional and trade qualification and licensure; but the dominance of these tests is explained by their other epithet, 'objective tests'. The strength of these tests is that they can provide fair or objective testing on a huge scale at small cost; fair in the sense that their administration is standardized and their developers can demonstrate, on the basis of quantitative, and therefore impressively legitimate data, that your results are not going to vary according to your marker. This, in turn, means that the results will stand up in court if challenged by a disgruntled candidate: a possibility with which test developers, universities, licensing boards and employers alike are obsessed in a country where litigation is rife.

American 'objective tests', which make the key hurdle for a practising nurse or teacher success on a battery of multiple-choice tests of information, are thus an extreme manifestation of far more general trends. In the UK, the recent introduction of national testing at ages 7, 11 and 14 (in addition to the pre-existing public examinations) brought to the fore disagreements about what assessment techniques were desirable or acceptable: disagreements which echo those surrounding competence-based assessment. Most curriculum and subject specialists advocated use of practical exercises and other forms of 'authentic' or 'performance' assessment by the teacher. However, such exercises were attacked as insufficiently fair and reliable, especially in view of the desire to use the results as 'objective' measures of school quality.

In this case, the attack on assessments by the teacher came from the political right, but there is actually nothing particularly right-wing, let alone 'conservative', about the basis of their critique. It is part of a far more general attack on the idea of 'traditional' authority and acceptance of professional judgement: the trend that has taken us away from the medieval 'master' towards machine-markable tests and computerized assessment batteries. A related development is the increased emphasis on accountability, which follows on the ever-rising level of expenditures on education and training. Further education, in particular, is facing demands that it demonstrate 'value added' – that students leave with more of something (qualifications? knowledge?) than when they arrived – and that institutions accept payment by results. Any significant shift to funding on this basis will almost inevitably bring with it an increased reliance on US-style testing which, however unsatisfactory in curriculum and content terms, is demonstrably 'fair' and cannot be manipulated by the colleges themselves.

The competence-based movement has been, from the start, extremely critical of the form most modern assessment takes. Yet in fact the movement itself encapsulates much of what we have just described. As we saw in Chapter 1, competence-based awards are characterized by attempts to make the criteria for success (or 'competence') completely explicit, a preoccupation with access and equal opportunity, and a rejection of the traditional authority of professional groups and assessors. It is competence-based awards, too, which have been made the subject of payment by results: Youth Training schemes receive more money if candidates pass NVQs than if they are failed. There is irony and tension here. As we discuss further below, in attempting to create systems which are transparent, 'rationally' justified by careful analysis, and proof against the fallibility of trainers and assessors, competency-based assessments tend to be driven further and further into replicating the atomized skill tests and 'knowledge' assessments which aroused such criticism in the first place.

Professional self-interest and credentialism

As was argued above, the trend towards formal, centralized and regulated assessment meshes with the self-interest of a large professional group: teachers and in particular teachers of students at and after compulsory leaving age. Teachers may not like to have the reliability of their professional judgement questioned and external controls introduced (in the form of centrally developed tests). However, at a more general level, anything that further increases the importance of formal educational qualifications as compared to other influences on people's life-chances has to benefit them as a group.

In modern industrial economies, ever-increasing levels of education are seen as a necessity. Comparative statistics about numbers of graduates, average length of schooling, vocational qualifications and the like are bandied around not only by academics and journalists but also by politicians of rival parties concerned to show that they are doing the most for 'national competitiveness'.

There is some considerable truth to this link between education and economic prosperity – but it is far more tenuous than most countries' politicians suppose. Japan may have the highest proportion of its age group staying in education till 18 years of any country in the world; but the Western European country with the lowest such figure is Switzerland – not noticeably a poor or failing economy, and one which contains some of the world's top companies in fields as diverse as pharmaceuticals, confectionery and engineering.

Detailed job analyses show that, in many cases, jobs which are reserved for graduates make no demands which can be clearly linked to the content or training of a university degree (Little 1984). Collins argues that education 'is not associated with employee productivity on the individual level, and job skills are learned mainly through opportunities to practice them' (Collins 1979: 48). Instead, he claims, education is a way of increasing one's relative competitive position, and inculcating people into professional cultures which exclude anyone who has not learned, during education, to speak the 'right' language. (See also Bourdieu and Passeron 1979; Bourdieu and Boltanski 1981.)

Similarly, longitudinal studies of graduate employment indicate that the major result of huge increases in the numbers completing higher education is that many jobs which were previously carried out by non-graduates have been redefined as graduate employment. This is not because the requirements of the jobs have changed appreciably, nor is there any evidence that graduate incumbents perform markedly better than their non-graduate elders. It is rather that employers who wanted to recruit from the top quarter of the population would, in the past, have felt sure of finding many such people among non-graduates. Now they feel that confining recruitment to graduates is the most efficient thing to do (Murphy 1993; Wolf 1993).

Academics bemoan expansion of student numbers to the extent that this involves declining resources per student; but expecting the education sector as a whole to question the value of its product would be asking a great deal! Self-interest is, of course, not the only reason why teachers encourage students to stay on at school or college, and academics praise the value of university study. Nonetheless, it is a fact that education needs customers if it is to stay in business. High demand for the products of education will increase its value, and the sector's ability to charge parents or the taxpayer for services rendered. Academics are, by and large, enthusiastic proponents of what has been called 'the Credential Society' (Collins 1979), and practise what they preach with such enthusiasm that in parts of the western world's university system it has become virtually impossible to hire eminent practitioners as teachers because they lack the necessary doctorate.

Qualification spirals, once they have started, tend to be self-fuelling for a long time. The more occupations become graduate entry, the more others feel under pressure to do so – to attract good entrants and for reasons of status and public respect. And the more this happens, again, the more individuals feel that they must obtain degrees. The same thing happens at other levels of the spiral – more A-levels, more certificated skills, more postgraduate diplomas.

Qualifications delivered by academic institutions will tend to be academic qualifications, because that is what the staff know about. If a university validates a course elsewhere – as part of a nursing degree, in a hospital, for example, or in a further education college – it is academic criteria and practices that will be required. That means, enough hours of theory, adequate demanding assignments of an academic nature suitable enough for higher education, and so on.

Academic institutions will vary in which parts of the market they cultivate, of course – Oxford University going for international managers and South Bank University (a former polytechnic) for London health visitors. But the trend is one that, inevitably, they welcome and encourage. And, once such courses are established, one then sees, again almost inevitably, academic drift within them.

Theoretical knowledge, academic criticism, discussion and the evaluation of language in written form and in debate are what academics know, and the domains in which they have succeeded themselves – the core values of the school and the academy.

These attributes are also what gain them status and prestige among their own peers. Within schools, Cookery becomes Food Studies, intent on analysing food values and designing question-naires on eating habits. At higher levels, new courses and subject areas are followed, soon after, by journals in which teachers of the subject can advance their careers by writing learned papers. More-over, within the system, quality-control mechanisms encourage more and more formal, paper-based approaches. Institutions are judged (and, in the UK, funded) in terms of their output of published material. The effective teaching of *practice* faces an uphill battle.

It is clear why academics might perpetuate this approach: but why do their employer clients? They could simply refuse to buy what the universities offer. There is nothing, in theory at least, to prevent a complete bifurcation between general education, based in schools, colleges and universities, and vocational training, based on the job. In practice, however, this becomes increasingly unlikely as modern economies develop. This is partly because of the traditional association of the 'higher professions' (law, medicine, religion) with universities, which gives the latter's qualifications and assessment methods a status to which employers are also not immune. Also important, though, are the nature of the modern economy itself, and the nature of modern government and the welfare state. Large companies are able to support specialized training programmes for entrants, but these are the concern of specialist departments, rather than executives, middle managers or senior skilled workers. Among small companies, very few feel able to provide anything like a coherent training programme (Vickerstaff 1991). This is partly a function of work pressure and organization. But it also reflects the fact that, in many cases, employees will be working in fairly specialized fields at any given time – but be expected to adapt at short notice to shifts in the firm's commercial environment and to workforce turnover. As discussed further in Chapter 4, this is proving a major obstacle to implement-ing the type of competence-based assessment envisaged by original architects of the English, NVQ approach.

Equally important, however, is the willingness of the state to pay for large parts of the vocational education and training system, notably for lawyers, accountants, engineers, plumbers and doctors. Why should an industry or profession take upon itself unnecessary costs when alternatives are on offer? The necessarily academic nature of university- and college-based training means, of course, that in many cases a final practice-based stage of training is required, and occupations vary in the balance which emerges: some engineering firms still spend large amounts on apprenticeship programmes as the only way to get the skilled people they need; lawyers spend time articled after preliminary qualifications. But financial incentives, varying from country to country but present throughout the world, give a further push towards academic routes into work.

This, then, is the context within which the competency-based assessment movement operates. What one must then ask is: does it matter? Is there any reason to suppose that an academic, knowledge-based approach to teaching vocational skills is necessarily a bad thing? Might it not, in fact, be just as good a preparation as any other?

The evidence, unfortunately, is overwhelmingly in the opposite direction. The next section reviews the relevant literature: the arguments from first principles, but also, more importantly, the empirical research findings.

What makes assessments valid?

We assess people because we want to make some sort of judgement about them – whether we talk about it in terms of skills, knowledge, competence or character. And the more information we have about them, the better able we are to make such a judgement. If we could follow a doctor around for the whole of his working life, and not only observe surgeries and home visits but also follow up on patients, we would be in a very good position to tell whether or not he or she was any good. Teachers are making the same point when they argue that they are in a better position than any single test can be to judge how a pupil is progressing (although they may not be in a very good position to know how pupils are doing compared to others in different parts of the country – and may also find it hard to be objective about all their pupils).

As a general rule, however, we make judgements on rather small amounts of evidence, which is why it is important that assessments should be as well designed as possible. This is particularly the case with assessments which matter a great deal either to the candidate (for example in deciding university entrance) or to the population as a whole (as with a large number of vocational qualifications which are taken to guarantee safe and 'competent' practice).

In vocational qualifications, we rely on assessments to make some quite specific but also far-ranging judgements about people's future behaviour. This means that, at a very general level, there are quite clear criteria for deciding if assessments are satisfactory: namely that they enable us to make such judgements soundly. Deciding whether or not a given assessment lives up to this task, however, may be a great deal less straightforward than this form of words suggests.

In fact, the advice on what sorts of assessment do satisfy requirements is so consistent that it tends almost to be treated as self-evident. It is that assessments must be judged by the extent to which the skills and behaviours which will ultimately be expected of candidates 'are reflected in the tasks presented to learners on a test' (Linn *et al.* 1991: 15). Vocational assessments – whether for driving instructors or clergymen – should be as close as possible to the reality of vocational practice.

As Nuttall has observed, an

> assessment is only valuable if the generalization we want to make holds up in practice, that is, in other circumstances or on other occasions. That is only likely if the sample of behaviour we assessed is a representative ... sample of the behaviour of interest.
>
> (Nuttall 1987)

Lindquist, one of the most eminent of American measurement specialists, was observing in 1951 that

> the most important consideration is that the test questions require the examinee to do the same things, however complex, that he is required to do in the criterion situations.
>
> (Lindquist 1951: 154)

This means the situations in which one is really interested. The logic underlying the advice is similarly 'self-evident'. As the quotations above indicate, assessment is often thought of as an example of sampling, in which we collect information about a subset of something in order to estimate what is going on overall. Quality control in a factory works like that. You test one item in every 100, or every 1000, as a way of checking whether products are up to standard. Similarly, in order to find out what opinions people hold about issues, pollsters ask questions of a sample of 500, 1000, or even 10 000.

If you want to estimate something on the basis of sampling of this type, you will get the best results if you sample directly the item you are interested in. Thus, if you want to know whether the brakes on an assembly line of cars are being fitted to standard, you test them, and not the gearbox. If you want to know what people think of a proposed policy (e.g. rail privatization) you ask them about that – and not some related matter such as bus services, motorway tolls, or the performance of the government overall. This argument generalizes easily enough to assessment. You do not (to take an ongoing controversy) test children's listening and speaking skills by means of a written comprehension test.

In the workplace 'assessment is valid when it registers accurately the presence of skills which convert directly into occupational competence' (Wood *et al.* 1989: 7). It follows that it is unlikely to be a good idea to qualify your accountants solely on the basis of rote memory tests and your social workers on their ability to write long academic essays. Nor is it sensible to make 30-minute panel interviews your main selection tool for any, far less all, jobs.

There is a general consensus among measurement experts that work samples, simulations, and what the competence movement refers to as 'performance assessments' will be better at measuring and predicting vocational skills than will paper-and-pencil tests (see for example Priestley 1982). Indeed, the basic tenets of competence-based assessment are an uncompromising statement of a position with which most measurement experts would have no theoretical disagreement.

> In competence-based assessment, it is individual performance which is judged – and judged against explicit standards which reflect ... the expected outcomes of that individual's competent performance ... If assessment uses explicit standards of occupational performance as its foundation, then the

logical way to assess whether someone is meeting those standards is to watch them working in that occupation.

(Fletcher 1991: 66–7)

The theoretical basis for the argument is set out clearly by Wernimont and Campbell (1968). They point out that psychologists'
interest is most often in using tests to provide 'signs' of some
(supposed) underlying trait or disposition – creativity, integrity,
intelligence. Too often assessment systems take the same indirect
approach to measuring and certifying candidates, and construct
composite scales of indirect measures when in fact 'the best
indicator of future performance is past performance' (ibid.: 172).
In other words, assessments which bear no resemblance to anything
anyone will do on the job are extremely unlikely, prima facie, to
be much use as predictors. Correspondingly, the best predictor
measures will be those which do incorporate parts of the future
behaviour which is of interest.

Looked at in this way, a very great deal of the assessment we
do comes out looking highly unsound. At the very least it lacks 'face
validity': it does not look as though it is doing what we want it
to. This is especially true, of course, with multiple-choice tests of
the type often used to license professionals in the United States, and
underlies the current American enthusiasm for 'authentic assessment'. As critics point out, no United States physician 'ever has to
answer complicated batteries of multiple-choice questions as a
routine part of his or her professional practice, even though their
competence evaluations are composed almost entirely of such
items' (McGaghie 1991: 6). Similarly in education, 'multiple-choice
tests of professional knowledge which are part of the licensing
requirements in 24 states, are not reliable measures of whether
applicants possess the knowledge to teach effectively' (Murnane
1991: 137). Nor can they be when 'the right answer to almost all
questions about how an effective teacher should respond in a particular classroom situation is "it depends"' (ibid.).

Outside the United States there are fewer targets as manifestly
lacking in face validity as the multiple-choice battery. Nonetheless,
there are plenty of grounds for criticism. For all the reasons
discussed above, there is heavy emphasis on the academic in vocational and professional courses and assessments. A bias towards
the testing of acquired knowledge is accompanied by a strong
resistance to assessing personal qualities and ability to deal with

people – areas which are difficult for academic institutions to handle for exactly the reasons that 'knowledge' is easy. And while practice situations generally are included in some way in assessments, they tend to cover a very narrow range.

All of this makes it easy to criticize and attack current practice from a more or less overtly 'competence-based' position. However, a critique is not, in itself, enough to justify (enforced) change. It is perfectly possible, for example, that authentic assessments would be better *if* they could be created – but that, in fact, they are impossible to carry out. It is possible, in other words, that this is a theoretical argument for which there is no empirical evidence at all. If so, one would do well to hesitate. Perhaps a proxy measure (such as academic performance over a wide range of subjects) might be better after all. The next section therefore reviews the empirical evidence in favour of assessments which set out to be as close to vocational reality as possible.

The empirical evidence

The relevant evidence falls into two groups: studies which look at the relationship between academic measures and occupational performance, and studies which relate occupational performance to work sample tests of various sorts, whether or not these are labelled as 'competence based'.

Academic measures and occupational performance

The evidence on the link between academic measures and vocational performance is almost consistently damning. One expert reviewer notes that

> Educational qualifications have long been favoured as a strong sign of potential success. It is believed that early academic endeavour must translate itself into later occupational endeavour. *The absence of any compelling evidence in support of such a belief has done nothing to dampen it.*
>
> (Wood 1991: 217; italics added)

One comprehensive review of the literature is that carried out by Samson and colleagues (1984) of research completed since 1950. This looked at studies which correlated performance on degree courses (including teaching and nursing) with an index of occupational performance since graduating. Zero correlation, (0.00 or a little above) would have meant that no relationship whatsoever could be found between one's degree performance and one's later occupational success; a correlation of 1.0 that relative occupational success could be predicted with absolute certainty on the basis of degree performance. Both alternatives are, of course, equally implausible, but the actual figures tend to be much closer to zero than to unity. While most studies showed some sort of positive correlation, the mean was only 0.155 and the median correlation was as low as 0.100.

The mean correlations for the studies examined were highest for nursing (0.26) and military/civil service occupations (0.23), followed by business, then teaching and engineering, while for medicine the mean correlation was not significantly different from zero. Only a very few studies produced figures much above or below these values, and the authors report the overall mean to be very much in line with other work undertaken by the US government on the relationship between college achievement and occupational success. It is also entirely consistent with older studies which, throughout this century, have suggested that the relationship between academic success at college and success in a profession is minimal.

These studies concerned *college* success (generally measured by Grade Point Average and involving American students). The evidence on pencil-and-paper occupational aptitude tests is generally similar. Aptitude tests are very often used either to select people for training programmes or as part of a firm's hiring policy. Some of them are very general indeed, and resemble the sort of verbal reasoning tests often used in schools. Others are intended to test for more specific aptitudes – mechanical, engineering, clerical. Wood concludes that, except for very large samples, there is actually 'less predictive power in a tailored composite battery of aptitude tests', supposedly oriented directly to the requirements of a particular job, than in a measure of general intelligence (Wood 1991: 221).

The most comprehensive review of such tests was undertaken by Ghiselli (1966). The median correlation with measures of occupational proficiency was 0.19, which the author characterized as 'far from impressive'. Gordon and Cohen (1973: 261) looked at psychological tests as a way of selecting people for training pro-grammes and also concluded that 'with the exception of a few studies, only modest success has been achieved in the prediction of trainability'.

More recently, Wigdor and Green (1991) reviewed the evidence available from US Armed Forces research on written tests, not of aptitude but of *knowledge*. One study examined relationships between hands-on performance measures and (a) specially con-structed 'school knowledge' tests, designed to cover domains which would also occur in training for the relevant occupations and (b) job knowledge tests, which also covered areas that might be dealt with during on-the-job training. As such, these knowledge tests stand half-way between supposedly general 'aptitude tests' and a fully competence-based approach, which would almost certainly incorporate hands-on measures.

Correlations for the job knowledge tests were much higher than those usually reported for studies involving pencil-and-paper tests, ranging from 0.35 for vehicle mechanics and 0.40 for the military police up to 0.73 for administrative specialists. School knowledge test scores consistently produced much lower correlations (though with the same occupations showing stronger or weaker relation-ships). However, even among the school knowledge tests, many correlations were higher than 0.3, and for medical specialists the correlation was 0.44, for administrative specialists 0.58. The higher correlations for some jobs probably reflect the relative importance of paper-based skills and 'recall' knowledge.

Wigdor and Green also report that, when evaluated carefully, various combinations of 'aptitude' questions can be identified which correlate quite highly with hands-on measures. However, the scale of research undertaken by the US Armed Forces for this purpose is far removed from that underpinning most supposed 'aptitude' measures.[9]

The issue of restricted range

There is one important reason why links between educational qualifications and future occupational performance are likely to appear quite tenuous, and which needs to be taken into account in weighing the evidence for and against various approaches. When studying people with a given qualification, one is only looking at a very small and specialized sub-sample of the population. If you link college grades of doctors to their future performance you are, by definition, only examining those who passed into, and out of, medical training successfully. The difference between those who got mostly As or mostly Bs on their medical examinations will clearly be tiny compared to the difference between both groups and either those who failed to qualify or the general population. The same applies to any professional or graduate group – just as it does to the (fairly low) correlation between grades on A-level examinations (taken when leaving school) and degree performance. If university entrance were completely open to anyone, then the link between A-level grades and degree performance would probably become a great deal higher.

At the same time, unpicking the relationship between different academic assessments also confirms that like relates to like. A-levels may not be great predictors of degree results, but they are better than any of the other ability, personality or motivational variables for which we have evidence (Smithers and Robinson 1989). They are markedly better than, for instance, aptitude tests, which are more different from degree examinations than are A-levels. A-level results are also better predictors of university success the closer and more direct is the link between the A-level syllabus and what is studied at university. Thus, for students reading science, maths or modern languages, A-levels predict success better than they do for psychology, sociology and engineering students (Choppin and Orr 1976).

Similar results emerge for further education. A study of the 'predictive value of CSE grades for further education' (Williams and Boreham 1971) found that, among 16-year-olds entering a variety of vocational courses, various combinations of grades from public examinations could provide quite good predictors of success. Once again, it was 'relevant' subjects that performed the best. Thus, maths, physics and technical drawing grades could be used quite effectively to predict whether someone would pass a technical/engineering course, whereas performance on shorthand typing and hairdressing courses was effectively unrelated to school success.

Nonetheless, even allowing for these relationships, the case against academic-style assessment as a way of predicting later vocational success is fairly strong. This, in turn, strengthens the theoretical case against it as the main basis for licensing and qualification – for predicting general competence as well as relative success. The next section summarizes the evidence which provides *positive* support for competence-style alternatives.

Work samples and the prediction of performance

Most of the relevant research findings in support of the 'competence' approach come from two sources: studies of craft and technician training schemes (generally of fairly short duration), and longitudinal studies of particular tightly knit occupational groups, who remain for long periods within the same organization, typically a large multinational, or a public organization such as the armed services, police or civil service. The reasons for this are logistical: namely that these are the only groups for whom it is possible to obtain 'occupational' measures of any consistency and reliability.

One of the criticisms made of the competency movement is that it tends to conceive of occupational training in an extremely mechanistic and atomistic way. Certainly the 'methodology' of competence-based assessment in England and Wales was developed in the context of training schemes concerned mostly with tightly defined semi-skilled and manual jobs. It is also the case that, for such jobs, the evidence in support of a 'work sample' approach to assessment is particularly strong.

In a review of what they called 'realistic' work sample tests Asher and Sciarrino (1974) demonstrated that such tests generally relate considerably more strongly to later success and proficiency measures than do paper-based 'aptitude' tests. This was particularly true for 'motor' tasks, involving the physical manipulation of things; rather less so for 'verbal' work sample tests involving language-oriented or 'people-oriented' tasks. Robertson and Kandola (1982) also report very high validity coefficients for work sample tests. Much of the work described involved tests to select the best candidates from among those already trained, but there is also a considerable literature on 'trainability testing' which involves predicting the capacity of applicants to learn the skill or job concerned. The approach is based directly on the arguments outlined above: that assessments should be as close as possible to the outcomes one is interested in, and that the best predictor of future performance is past performance. Trainability tests therefore involve giving people a small amount of specific early training in the relevant area, and then asking them to perform the relevant task unaided.

Trainability tests have been used quite extensively in the UK, notably with government retraining programmes. Downs (1970), who has been most widely involved in their development and evaluation, notes that a learning task which is to be used in such an assessment, needs to (a) be based on crucial elements on the job, (b) use only such skill and knowledge as can be imparted during the learning period, (c) be sufficiently complex to allow a range of observable errors to be made and (d) be carried out in a reasonable time.

The overlap between the philosophy of trainability testing and the more general tenets of a 'competence-based' approach make the results of trainability studies particularly interesting. A survey article of research results on UK trainability tests (Robertson and Downs 1979) summarizes correlations for trainees where entry into training was not made dependent on the test result. Correlations with final ratings at the end of training for 16 such studies show that there were only two cases where the relationship did not reach conventional significance levels. Correlations for the others ranged from 0.37 to 0.81, with a mean value of 0.52 and a median value of 0.50.

These are obviously considerably more impressive figures than those found for occupational aptitude tests. None the less some caveats are in order. The training courses for which the tests were developed were all of fairly short duration – typically around three months. Robertson and Downs (1979: 49) note that, in general, 'the predictive value of trainability tests does attenuate over time ... and such tests may be most valuable for short duration (e.g. six months or less) courses'. The courses studied were also ones that trained people in a number of highly specific skills, in which a 'point to point correspondence' between test and ultimate outcome was therefore feasible, and a test of this type had very strong face validity. The approach may not generalize nearly as successfully to broader skills.

Smith (1991) comes to similar conclusions. Tightly defined work sample and trainability tests are most suited to highly specific training programmes, he suggests, or to predicting fairly short-term performance in specific applied fields. They are less likely to be appropriate in selecting people for very general training, or for areas in which outcomes cannot be defined in a highly specific fashion – issues which, as we shall see below, pose problems for the wider ranging and more ambitious competency-based approach in its turn.

The other major source of evidence on competence-type approaches is longitudinal studies of occupational success. The groups for whom one can relate good, standardized early measures of *job-related* performance to later success are, obviously enough, few in number: in practice, as noted above, managers with some large corporations and public service employees (police, armed forces, civil service). All of these groups run centralized training and assessment centres, and retain their employees long enough for longitudinal tracking to be possible.

The largest single body of evidence relates to assessment centres run by large companies with the express view of measuring management 'potential'. They are institutions set up for internal training and selection purposes, and carry out careful analysis of a particular firm's management structure and demands before devising assessments based on these. Overall 'scores' from assessment centres are generally quite strongly correlated with later success within the institution, as measured by promotion and later salary. The relationship is strongest 5–10 years after centre attendance. The scores also positively related to peer and subordinate ratings of the manager concerned (see for example, Mitchell 1975; Wingrove *et al.* 1985; McEvoy and Beatty 1989). Correlations in both cases are typically between 0.3 and 0.6. Some critics have argued that this may be just a self-fulfilling prophecy, viz. that people do well *because* they have been given a high rating by the assessment centre. There is probably some truth to this – if a firm spends a great deal on such centres it has a strong incentive to take note of what they report. However, studies which have measures of later performance other than promotion (e.g. peer and subordinate ratings) also show strong positive relationships with centre ratings, albeit lower than for promotion. Overall, it seems clear that these assessments do have some substantial validity as measures and predictors of success in managerial jobs (Klimoski and Brickner 1987; Wolf and Silver 1990).

As one might expect, the less unified and centralized the corporate culture, the less successful the centres are at predicting later performance. This is probably partly because one has lost the 'self-fulfilling' element of the relationship: the fact that, as noted above, people who do well in assessment centre tests are more likely to be promoted as a result of their centre performance. However, it is also because the assessments themselves are likely to be less tightly modelled on the organization's requirements. Since only a small proportion of the population works in large, highly uniform organizations, this implies problems for competency-style testing to which we return in Chapter 4.

None the less, results from less centralized organizations do, again, provide strong support for the basic premise, viz. that 'competence-style' assessments have a demonstrable validity in measuring occupational performance which academic and psychological tests lack. The longest-term studies in the literature are British: a 19-year Cabinet Office study of a police assessment centre, serving a large number of independent police forces, each with their own appraisal systems and a 25-year follow up of Royal Navy selection procedures (Gardner and Williams 1973; Feltham 1988a,b). The Cabinet Office data showed positive relationships between assessment centre performance and later success, albeit lower than in firm-specific centres, with particularly strong relationships to some (not all) of the work-sample type tests. The Royal Navy data included results on a very wide range of written tests (though not direct work samples), including memory for design, maths and physics. Results were strongly correlated with success in training, and there were also positive and significant relationships with career position 20 years later, although by that time the size of the link was, not surprisingly, quite low.

Overall, then, the evidence provides considerable support at a theoretical level for the competence-based approach. Arguing from first principles, we can conclude that faithful simulation and sampling of the behaviour of interest should provide us with the most valid form of assessment. To this it can be added that evidence from places which have taken such an approach confirms its advantages, in terms of predictive validity, over more conventional methods. However, as we have mentioned, most such evidence comes from rather specialized contexts: short-term skills courses, or assessments for a stable corporate culture. In Chapters 3 and 4 we look at the issues raised when we move from such contexts to attempts at nationwide implementation, and evaluate the likelihood of success on this far wider scale.

3

THEORETICAL ISSUES IN A CRITERION-BASED SYSTEM

In discussing the origins of competence-based assessment, we have noted the overlap between the assumptions of competence-based and criterion-referenced assessment and suggested that competence-based assessment is most usefully seen as a particular type of criterion-referenced system (see p. 3). This overlap has, indeed, been recognized quite explicitly by the architects of the British competence-based approach, although they would argue that their system represents an elaboration and improvement on criterion-referencing rather than simply a variant. Gilbert Jessup, for example, in internal documents which elaborated on the basic call for 'standards' in the New Training Initiative, argued explicitly that what were needed were 'criterion-referenced standards', and drew the conventional contrast between the nature of a criterion-referenced system and 'current practice in accreditation, where performance is judged in relation to the performance of other trainees' (Jessup 1985: reprinted in Jessup 1991: 165–73).

In evaluating the effects which competence-based systems have had on vocational education, we will be discussing how far, in fact, competence-based assessment is free of 'norms' or judgements made in relation to others' performance. In this chapter, however, we focus more directly on the methodology of competence-based and criterion-referenced assessment as such, and on the theoretical assumptions which all such assessment systems share.

In the UK, the assessment of competence-based qualifications has become synonymous with the use of large numbers of very detailed and specific performance criteria. What this means, in effect, is that competence-based assessment is presented by its proponents as requiring a very specific assessment methodology. This methodology is also more or less universally adopted for all 'criterion-referencing'. Correspondingly, it is believed that it can provide – indeed, that its use guarantees – information about a candidate's competence (skills, knowledge, etc.) that is *substantive and specific, and highly reliable*. In this chapter, we look at how far such a claim can be justified. The first part of the chapter looks at whether the definitions on which this form of assessment rests – 'statements of competence' or 'performance criteria' – really can live up to the claims made for them. The second part then examines how far this approach solves the problems of assessor judgement.

Performance criteria and domain specification

The 'performance criteria' of American competency-based education, and the more elaborate structure of standards-based National Vocational Qualifications (NVQs) can both be seen as examples of a more general category: the domain specification. Any form of criterion-referenced assessment concerns itself with a highly specific 'domain' of behaviour, whether this be an aspect of occupational competence or an academic outcome. This, indeed, is their claim to superiority, whether the comparison is made with established vocational qualifications driven by classroom tradition and academic concerns, or with 'norm-referenced' academic tests which tell one only where a candidate stands relative to others. W. J. Popham, the doyen of criterion-referenced testing, gives this definition:

> A criterion-referenced test is used to ascertain an individual's status with respect to a well-defined behavioral domain.
>
> (Popham 1978)

This idea of a well-defined domain encapsulates the appeal of a 'competence based' system, and is the keystone of any system based on the achievement of 'criteria'. For the system to deliver on its promises, this domain needs to be specified in such a clear and unambiguous way that anyone involved in assessment will know exactly what to do (see for example, Berk 1984; Cronbach 1990). In academic contexts, the relevant audience may be writers of test items rather than teachers themselves. In competence-based assessment of a vocational or professional nature, assessors will be far more numerous. For both, the specification process is the key. It determines how meaningful and attainable a one-to-one match between assessment and domain actually is. Can one, in fact, use it to generate tests or assessments which provide well-founded, substantive information about individuals – and do so again and again, for vastly different 'domains' and myriad candidates?

Any testing manual dealing with criterion-referenced test construction starts with the specification of 'domain descriptions'. In current competence-based assessment, the parallel is exact. The 'standards' on which NVQs are based are intended to be so precise that they convey exactly what an assessor should look for. Jessup, for example, argues that provided 'assessments conform to the requirements in the elements of competence and their performance criteria' they will automatically be valid and being 'valid will necessarily be comparable and thus reliable' (Jessup 1991: 192).

None the less, as we saw in Chapter 1, this goal of precision has proved elusive. In pursuit of it, English competence-based awards have become ever more complex in structure, and ever more weighted down with detail. This is not because of some problem specific to competence-based assessment or NVQs in particular. On the contrary. Once we see them as examples of a 'criterion-referenced' approach, we can also see that this ever-receding goal of total clarity derives not from bad luck or incompetence, but is actually inherent in the methodology adopted. The more serious and rigorous the attempts to specify the domain being assessed, the narrower and narrower the domain itself becomes, without, in fact, becoming fully transparent. The attempt to map out free-standing content and standards leads, again and again, to a never-ending spiral of specification.[10]

If the claims of a criterion-referenced system are to hold, then domain descriptions or standards must exist in an unambiguous, unproblematic one-to-one relationship with the actual process of assessment. As Hambleton and Rogers (1991) put it in assessment-speak: 'Stringent adherence to domain or item specifications . . . is essential in constructing criterion-referenced tests because the resulting scores are referenced back to the item specifications at the interpretation stage.' In other words, since we are going to use the test to make statements about someone's concrete abilities in a particular area, the two had better match up exactly. If they do not, in fact, have this relationship then we cannot use the results of the assessment to make a definitive statement about someone's behaviour (or competence).

Confidence in the ability of the specification to guide the assessor is especially apparent in competence-based systems. In more academic versions of criterion-referencing (see below), the specification tends actually to lay down the parameters of the test instrument in considerable detail. Standards used for NVQs, by contrast, tend to pay rather little attention to this – though they may lay down more general requirements for the nature and frequency of assessment taking place. The training of NVQ assessors is concerned with the mechanics of using standards, recording performance and the like: the interpretation and application of particular standards are seen as quite unproblematic.

The same situation holds true for the 'external verifiers' from the awarding bodies, who check on the quality of assessments being carried out. Their main concern is for 'centres' (usually further education colleges) to demonstrate how their general assessment programme caters for the various criteria and requirements of the standards: in other words, to show that (*not* how) every performance criterion and every element of the range matches up with some form of assessment and has not been forgotten. There is generally no check on the administration and level of the assessment itself, instructions for which are assumed to be 'carried' by the standards specification.

Unfortunately, this keystone of criterion-referencing, in its currently understood form, crumbles at the touch. Any check on whether definitions do indeed map directly onto assessments leads us into ever tighter definitions, ever narrower domains. And even then, however hard we try, the domain specifications cannot carry all the information we require. Ambiguity remains.

All this can best be understood by looking at examples. In order to demonstrate how far this is a problem of all criterion-referenced

Objective
The student will be able to find the name of a point between 0 and 1 on the number line.

Directions and sample test item
Read the problem carefully and choose the correct answer. Place the letter beside your answer on the answer sheet next to the number of the problem.

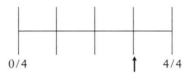

Find the number which correctly replaces the pointer in the number line above.

(a) 3   (b) $1\frac{3}{4}$ (c) $\frac{3}{4}$ (d) $\frac{1}{4}$

Content section
1 The student is given a number line with endpoints labelled zero and one.
2 The divisions on the line shall be equally spaced.
3 The number of divisions on the line will be a multiple of the given denominator.
4 A pointer is used to identify the unknown point on the line.

Response section
1 There are one correct and three incorrect responses.
2 The responses are given in ascending or descending order.
3 The distractors shall include:
  (a) the numeral which represents the ordinal position of the point in question;
  (b) the numeral which represents the length of each division on the number line; and
  (c) the numeral which is one more than the correct response.

Figure 3.1 An 'exemplary' domain specification.
Source: Hambleton and Zaal (1991)

systems rather than specific to its 'competence-based' variant, the first example given relates to a traditional academic task. Figure 3.1 reproduces a domain specification, promoted as 'exemplary' by criterion-referencing specialists[11] concerned to make clear whether a student has mastered a particular academic objective or skill. The level of detail is daunting: all this for one small, discrete part of basic arithmetic. But does it, in fact, achieve its purpose?

Almost certainly not. The correct answer in the example given is $\frac{3}{4}$. Has a candidate who gives this response really shown that they can 'find the name of a point between 0 and 1 on the number line', though? If we look at the detailed instructions to the test writer, we find at once that the items allowed are far from being all those that might be involved in 'finding a point between 0 and 1'. First of all, the line provided has to be divided into equally spaced divisions, e.g. quarters, fifths, eighths, thus excluding any questions in which the candidate has to figure out, from the scale, which divisions are being shown. Then, most of the alternative answers are to reflect the way the line is divided, so that, if it is divided up into eighths, the test cannot deal with quarters and halves. Not only the nature of the alternatives offered is predefined, so is the order in which they are to be presented. One cannot offer the candidate the choice between '$\frac{3}{4}$; 3; $\frac{1}{4}$; $1\frac{3}{4}$', but only between '3; $1\frac{3}{4}$; $\frac{3}{4}$; $\frac{1}{4}$'.

What this means, of course, is that we cannot safely use the test to state whether someone can 'find the name of a point between 0 and 1' at all. With an incompletely divided line, or alternatives in a different order, or different sorts of alternatives, or a non-multiple-choice format, they might not be able to name the point. On the other hand, the test specification had good reason for being so restrictive. Studies of assessment invariably show that test questions which authors think are approximately equal in difficulty, or test the same domain, actually prove very different indeed in how difficult they are, and in the skills and competences which people actually call on when answering them.[12] A very detailed study by Pollitt *et al.* (1985) *What Makes Examination Questions Difficult?* demonstrated that in each subject, there are characteristics which make supposedly 'equivalent' tasks or questions more or less difficult – but also that these are highly subject-specific and *very difficult to predict in advance.*[13]

Seen in this light, the enormously restrictive nature of the 'number line' example is understandable. The writers want to be sure that the test items generated by assessors really are equivalent in difficulty and really are testing the same things. A test which gives possible answers in a 'muddled up' way may be harder (or easier) than one where they are in ascending or descending order. A test without a distractor which is 'one more than the correct response' may be easier than the alternative ... and so on.

Even this specification may not have avoided the trap: a test dealing mostly with quarters (like our example) or with thirds and eighths, might be very different in difficulty from one dealing with ninths, elevenths and thirteenths. But it does at least narrow the differences down. Given the specification, no one will assess using a format other than multiple choice, let alone start embedding 'number value' questions in a problem. Simply leaving it to people to assess 'number line skills' as they saw fit would unquestionably produce different formats, different contexts, different types of problem, and 'criterion judgements' about someone's competence which would be very different indeed in what they implied. The trouble is that, in seeking to pre-empt such variety in assessment tasks, this specification reaches a point of ridiculous restrictiveness, and yet *still* fails to ensure that there is a one-to-one correspondence between assessment and objective.

It is worth emphasizing that the mathematics test specification, while offered as exemplary, is also in its general features typical of US experience in creating criterion-referenced tests. In the United States, the approach has tended to produce very narrowly defined tests, largely multiple choice. This is not an unfortunate co-incidence. On the contrary, it follows from the identification of 'criterion-referencing' with a particular, seductive, and apparently tightly theorized philosophy of domain specification and test construction. For its proponents, 'the heart of criterion-referenced measurement is that it provides additional meaning from scores by referencing the test outcome to a clearly specified body of test content, *from which the items are generated*' (Millman 1984: italics added). Abandon that, the test constructors would argue, and you have abandoned the whole claim of criterion-referencing to generate clear statements about candidates' performance in a domain.

There is a tendency among some 'criterion-referencing' enthusiasts to respond to these sorts of problems and findings by calling for yet more detail, yet more specificity. It is therefore worth finishing this section by returning to James Popham himself:

> Once upon a time, when I was younger and foolisher, I thought we could create test specifications so constraining that the test items produced as a consequence of their use would be functionally homogeneous, that is, essentially

interchangeable. But if we use the difficulty of an item as at least one index of the item's nature, then it becomes quite obvious that even in such teensy behaviour domains as measuring the student's ability to multiply pairs of double-digit numbers, the task of $11 \times 11 = ?$ is lots easier than $99 \times 99 = ?$ About the only way we can ever attain functional homogeneity is to keep pruning the nature of the measured behaviour so that we're assessing ever more trifling sorts of behaviour. That would be inane.

(Popham 1984: 39)

Vocational applications

Few competence-based systems would endorse domains and criteria as narrow as the example we have just discussed. Indeed, while, as we have seen, NVQs have in fact consistently moved towards greater and greater attempts at specificity, many advocates of a competence-based approach would explicitly reject this as self-defeating. Nonetheless, any competence-based system ultimately faces the same dilemmas. However broadly defined its criteria, the objective – and the claim – is that these are clearly defined in such a way that the assessor can describe a candidate as having unambiguously achieved (or 'not yet achieved') them. As Johnson expressed it, 'The criterion of success is demonstration of ability to do the job. Mastery criteria are used to determine how well students perform. These criteria must be met for students to be considered competent' (Johnson 1974). The requirement is thus for a one-to-one relationship between criteria and competence, and between assessment and criteria – just as with the number line, and with just as much elusiveness.

Many of the performance criteria in competence-based qualifications are almost as narrow as the examples furnished by academic criterion-referenced tests. A Level 2 NVQ in Business Administration is one of the largest NVQs in terms of entries, since it is very well suited to training and accrediting specific office skills. It is one of the few NVQs which is quite easy to assess in the workplace; it is delivered in a large number of Youth Training schemes involving work experience plus skills training and it is also taken by considerable numbers of full-time students in further education. Tables 3.1 and 3.2 illustrate an element concerned

Table 3.1 Version One of a Level 2 Business Competence ('Identify and retrieve documents from within an established filing system')

Performance criteria
(a) Specified documents are promptly located, extracted and passed to correct person or location.
(b) Delays in the supply of files and/or documents are notified and reasons for delay politely explained.
(c) All file and document movements are correctly recorded, up to date and legible.

Range statement
The Competence includes paper-based filing systems covering the retrieval of information from alphabetical and numerical filing systems, involving indexing systems and lateral and vertical filing methods. It requires competence in booking in and out procedures and the tracing of missing or overdue files.

Underpinning knowledge and skills
(a) Identifying and interpreting classification systems.
(b) Classifying documents.
(c) Procedures and systems of organisation, including special and confidential files and retention policy.
(d) Importance of effective control and retrieval of information.
(e) Filing and indexing systems (e.g. alphabetical, numerical).
(f) Filing methods (e.g. lateral, vertical).
(g) Booking out and bring forward systems.
(h) Planning and organizing work within deadlines.

Specific assessment guidance
It is preferable for assessment of this competence to be carried out in the workplace over a period of time. If simulation is the only method available, students must demonstrate competence by dealing consecutively with a minimum of 20 items to be extracted, on a minimum of three separate occasions. *Ad hoc* contingencies must be introduced which require students to re-allocate priorities. A completely different set of documents must be provided for each simulated assessment.

Source: BTEC First Diploma in Business and Finance, designed to deliver National Vocational Qualification at Level 2: 1991 version of standards

Table 3.2   Version Two of a Level 2 Business Competence ('Obtain information from an established storage system')

Performance criteria
(a) Required information is promptly located, obtained and passed to correct person or location.
(b) Delays in the supply of information are notified and reasons for delay politely explained.
(c) Information obtained is correctly recorded, up to date and in the required form.
(d) Missing or overdue items are identified and correct procedures followed to locate them.

Range statements
Methods of classifying information:
• alphabetical
• numerical

Knowledge/understanding
• classification systems and their identification and interpretation
• methods of classifying information
• storage and indexing systems
• storage methods
• booking out and bring forward systems
• organizational storage systems and practices including special and confidential information

---

Source: City & Guilds Business Administration NVQ (Level 2), 1994 version of standards

essentially with filing. It comes in two forms, involving two different awarding (examining) bodies, but also two consecutive versions of the standards: both examples are from accredited NVQs, and so reflect directly standards content and format.

Once again, what is striking is not only the level of detail but the way in which additional requirements simply occasion new queries. Does it matter what sort of alphanumeric system is used? Will the assessment be to the same standard if documents come from systems containing 20 files, rather than 2000? How correctly is correctly? How legible is legible? And so on ...

Many competence statements, however, are of a far broader kind – intentionally so. The competence movement, in the United States, the UK and Australia has always paid attention to the

Table 3.3 Element for a Higher Level NVQ (from Training &
Development Lead Body Standards)

B113   Agree a strategic plan which meets organisational requirements
(a) Proposals are presented which match the implementation of agreed
strategy to organizational requirements and priorities.
(b) Proposals identify accurately when outcomes critical to
organisational requirements are to be achieved.
(c) Responsibilities for achievement of, and support for, the plan are
clearly defined.
(d) Proposals are based on agreed organisational development and
resourcing strategies and plans.
(e) Proposals are produced within agreed timescales and budgets.
(f) Decision-makers are given adequate opportunities to ask questions
and seek clarification.
(g) Negotiations and agreements are conducted and concluded in a
manner which preserves goodwill and trust.
(h) Agreed plans are summarized accurately and made available to
those who require this information.

Range indicators

Types of plan:	written/oral; free standing/part of a corporate planning system.
Relationship with decision-makers:	peers/subordinates/superiors; employers/employees/clients.
Presentation methods:	oral, written, audio-visual, computer-based.
Presentation/negotiation processes:	direct/face to face; remote/via technology-based systems.

---

importance of broad conceptions of what 'competence' involves –
insisting that 'competence is a wide concept', embracing transfer,
planning, personal effectiveness and not merely narrow skills. The
examples in Tables 3. 3 and 3.4 are thus expressly drawn from the
less 'narrow' end of the extant spectrum. The example in Table 3.3
is taken from the Training and Development Lead Body Standards,
designed for the trainers and educators who actually deliver and
assess NVQs, and developed with direct NCVQ involvement. That
in Table 3.4 is from a set of competence-based requirements which
are not NVQs (and not expected to become so). Both deal with
broad competencies; both form part of qualifications which, at

Table 3.4   Sample Health Visitor Competence

---

3   *Health Visiting Practice: 'Services for individuals and families'*
At the end of Supervised Practice the student should be able to:
(i)   identify individuals, families and groups requiring help and support, taking into account physical, psychological and social needs;
(ii)   monitor the health and developmental progress of children of all ages, referring as appropriate;
(iii)   monitor the health and progress of adults including the elderly;
(iv)   plan health goals for, and in cooperation with, individuals, families and groups;
(v)   formulate, implement and evaluate health visiting programmes in relation to identified goals;
(vi)   establish and maintain a pattern of home visiting;
(vii)   mobilize resources, refer to other agencies;
(viii) facilitate self-help groups;
(ix)   organize and participate in clinic sessions.

---

the end, are expected to inform the world that the successful candidate 'can do' the things concerned.

Thus, whatever the level, the assumption is that the assessors will not find the actual assessment task problematic. The specifications will allow them to move from 'item specifications' to interpretation and description, and back again, without ambiguity. Confidence in the ability of standards to convey clear meaning underpins the confident speed with which new competence-based qualifications have been introduced in the UK. It also inheres in the way assessor training has been designed. As noted elsewhere, NCVQ encourages (and in the future will require) NVQ assessors to obtain 'assessor awards', as part of its quality-control programme. These awards, however, are concerned with the general process of NVQ assessment and not with acquiring occupation-specific expertise. The latter is assumed to be held already, and simply clarified by the benchmarks which standards provide.

What is being assumed and relied upon, in other words, is a pre-existing consensus and understanding on the part of the assessors. That assumption itself implies another, from which, indeed, the whole of competence-based assessment starts, namely that there *exist* 'standards of competence' for an industry or role. The assumption that these can then be articulated clearly through written documents is secondary. The documents do not, in theory, create the standards. Rather, they articulate and clarify them to professionals who can understand them *because* of their prior knowledge and implicit understanding of what 'competence' in their own context means. Thus standards developers will explain that one goes on defining 'as long as it is necessary. You stop when everyone understands' (Personal communication). Given the underlying assumption of shared knowledge, this is a perfectly coherent position; but it does rest on that basic assumption holding up.

If we take a critical attitude towards the standards reproduced in Tables 3.3 and 3.4, it is easy to show that they do not begin to provide item specifications so tight that any novice could use them to construct parallel assessments. In the training and development element, for example, how is one to recognize that 'proposals identify accurately' when critical outcomes are to be achieved, or understand what 'agreed resourcing strategies and plans' are meant to be? Can a shared occupational culture really make the requirements unambiguous, so that the endless spiral of specification which, we argued, was always attendant on criterion-referencing is broken by the existence of shared expertise?

It must be said that there has been very little independent evaluation of whether standards are implemented in any comparable or consistent way. Indeed, it would be rather difficult to do this at all clearly. By nature, those using them in workplaces will be dealing with very different contexts, so it is not clear how we would measure 'sameness' precisely. None the less, we must seriously question whether it is likely even in principle that a combination of definitions and prior consensus will produce any very uniform behaviour. We must also wonder whether the assumption of pre-existing 'standards' and shared understanding is reasonable at all. We noted in Chapter 1 that, in England, one of the motives behind the introduction of a competence-based system, and the establishment of lead bodies, was to improve the quality of training, and to spread best practice throughout an industry. But if lead body definitions have, as one of their objectives, the encouragement of *change* in people's conceptions, it is obviously unwise to predicate our assessment system on the assumption that conceptions are stable and uniform.

Certainly, such evidence as exists is not terribly encouraging. Harry Black and his colleagues at the Scottish Council for Research in Education (SCRE) studied in detail the way in which a number of colleges were delivering apparently quite specific Stock Control modules within the Scottish National Certificate, which, as we saw in Chapter 1 (p. 8), was the first national (Scottish) qualification to embody competence-based approaches in a consistent way. All the departments were experienced and had close ties with local industry and the colleges themselves assumed that the Stock Control modules would be quite easy to deliver to a common standard. In fact, however, both content and standards deviated greatly within the group (Black *et al.* 1989).

Compared to the National Certificate modules, NVQ developments have involved greater specification, greater restrictions on format, longer lists, tighter definitions. In research sponsored by the Manpower Services Commission as part of their early work on standards (Wolf and Silver 1986), we asked experienced college tutors and workplace supervisors to devise exercises based on very detailed 'standard tasks'. In spite of the shared occupational culture of the individuals concerned, the assessment items they produced, following these specifications, proved to be very different in content.

We also looked at the level of difficulty at which the assessors ascribed mastery, by asking them to administer and make judgements using a more standardized 'anchor test' at the same time as they used their own. The standard at which they ascribed 'competence' on this common exercise turned out to be markedly different – implying that the underlying standard being applied to the different, and therefore not directly comparable, exercises of their own was also highly variable. Similar results were obtained with tourist guide examiners operating out of different regional offices, even though they had mostly done their own training together, and operated an external examiner system which created some cross-region links (Wolf 1994; see also Chapter 4 for a more detailed discussion).

Reports back to NCVQ about comparability problems have, as we discussed, encouraged the Council to create ever-longer, more restrictive standards, in an attempt to create uniformity by central control. And so the minutiae pile up and the domain shrinks – without, in fact, guaranteeing the precise equivalence of assessment

items at all. In general, the verdict seems clear. Written specifications, on their own, leave large areas of ambiguity and cannot
deliver on the more inflated claims made for them. To understand
in more detail why this is the case, the next section looks at the
core of any assessment: the judgement of the assessor.

Assessor judgement

The problems with domain specification discussed in the previous
section are increasingly recognized – both in the theoretical literature and among people actually trying to implement competence-
based systems. Less attention has been given to issues of assessor
judgement. We can argue, however, that they are at least as important for a competence-based approach, and potentially quite as
threatening to its ambitions and objectives. There are two major
issues which are of particular importance for competence-based
awards, and which have a direct impact on the way assessors
operate: (1) the inherently high variability in the context of assessment, and (2) the way in which assessments and evidence are
aggregated to reach a final judgement about whether competence
has been achieved.

Any form of assessment involves activity and judgement on the
assessor's part – whether it be examining a PhD, listening to a
music examination candidate, observing a care assistant or even
marking a multiple-choice paper. (Candidates have an uncanny
knack of missing the boxes when they make their marks.) All the
research evidence that we have on assessors' behaviour emphasizes
the very active role that their own concepts and interpretations play
(see for example, Gipps and Wood 1981; Wolf and Silver 1986;
Pollard *et al.* 1994). Assessors do not simply 'match' candidates'
behaviour to assessment instructions in a mechanistic fashion. On
the contrary: they operate in terms of an internalized, holistic
set of concepts about what an assessment 'ought' to show, and
about how, and how far, they can take account of the context of
the performance, make allowances, refer to other evidence about
the candidate in deciding what they 'really meant', and so on.
For example, assessors will 'make allowances' for whether or not
a question or task was particularly difficult in evaluating a
candidate's response. An Associated Board music examiner,

listening to the performance of a piece, will operate with a holistic model in which accuracy, rhythm and dynamics are all important, but where lapses in one can be offset by strengths elsewhere. The more complex the behaviour the more this type of process comes into play.

For example, current GCSE mathematics examinations require candidates to complete a number of open-ended 'investigations'. In the early stages of the GCSE, most boards asked examiners to score each investigation on a number of separate criteria, such as 'elaboration'. However, this proved to be unworkable (Wolf 1990). Although there was no disagreement in the teaching/examining community about the importance of the criteria, some tasks turned out to encourage demonstrations of one outcome, some another. Was a candidate to be penalized for that? If the logic of a problem implied strong development in one area and not in another, how could one reasonably operate with a mark scheme which made high overall marks impossible except where all areas were developed equally? Instead, the boards have, for the most part, moved to asking for an overall judgement on the investigations, with it being left to the assessor how the various components are combined.

The parallels with competence-based assessment are quite close here. Just as the investigations differed in their contexts, demands and opportunities, making a single strict mark scheme inappropriate, so, too, will there be differences in the contexts and demands of workplace activities being used to assess different candidates.

Discussions of competence-based assessment often imply that assessor judgement is only a minor issue because the assessment criteria are so minutely and clearly specified that one is well down towards the more mechanistic end of the spectrum, closer to multiple-choice testing than examining a Grade 8 piano candidate. 'Individual performance . . . is judged against explicit standards . . . and individuals know exactly what they are aiming to achieve' (Fletcher 1991: 66). Assessment is believed to require far less in the way of complex judgement than with the opaque criteria employed by traditional school-based or higher education.

In fact, nothing could be further from the truth. The inherent variability of the contexts in which competence is tested and displayed means that assessors have to make constant, major decisions. They must determine how to take account of context when judging whether an observed piece of evidence fits a defined

criterion. In other words, they operate with a compensating procedure which itself requires an internalized, holistic model – not a
simple set of atomized domain descriptors (see for example,
Christie and Forrest 1981; Cresswell 1987; Brehmer 1989).

We can see this process at work by considering the actual process
by which one devises assessments. What happens in practice,
especially on higher-level courses involving external (often further
education- or higher-education-based) assessors, is that the latter
in effect throw the standards away – or more accurately, shelve
them for much of the time and start again from the overall concepts. Imagine yourself involved in a Management Charter
Initiative (MCI) qualification, a standards-based management
qualification (perhaps an MBA) offered through the Government-
backed MCI. You will have to amass evidence that you can meet
a large number of performance criteria, much of it, inevitably,
gathered via project and simulation work since few managers are
(or should be) in a position to tackle every part of the standards
in their current job. 'Element I 6.2' forms part of one MCI 'key
role': *Manage people.* The element's title is *Plan activities and
determine work methods to achieve objectives* and typical performance criteria are 'The degree of direction required by individuals
is accurately assessed and used to best effect in overall work planning', and 'Where possible, decisions on work and methods include
suggestions from those involved.'

Faced with these criteria, what a tutor/assessor can do, and in
practice does, is to read through the standards for general meaning,
and identify that their concern is with detailed planning of how to
use and motivate a team of very different individuals in carrying
out a complex task. He or she will then set an assignment or create
a simulated situation involving some such objective and set of people, and typically, assess it in a holistic way as satisfactory (competent) or not. Only then, at the very end, when the task is complete,
will the performance criteria be re-examined in detail – and then
only in order to see if there is any area which has not been touched
on at all, and so cannot, really, be 'ticked off'.

Throughout this process, there are obviously a great many
complex judgements being made by the assessor. However, it is not
clear that many of these derive from the standards. The key
judgements have far more to do with whether someone has actually
performed up to the *assessor's* standards than with the individual

performance criteria at all.[14] And whether or not one assessor applies standards which are the same as another's will also, in a case like this, have rather little to do with the focus on competence and outcomes.

The point is not that decentralized assessors cannot assess to an acceptably common standard. They can, but the process is complex, incremental and, above all, judgemental. *It has to be because the actual performance which one observes – directly, or in the form of artefacts – is intrinsically variable:* one person's playing of a piano piece, one person's operations plan, is by definition not exactly the same as another's, and cannot be fitted mechanistically to either a written list of criteria, or to an exemplar. Thus, simply sending instructions into classrooms or workplaces, even ones where the trainers and teachers share a strong common culture, can only get one so far – and not what most people would regard as far enough.

Up to now, we have been discussing judgement and 'compensation' (making allowances) at the level of individual judgement. In the case of academic testing, the judgements may simply be given at this individual discrete level, though even here it is rare. In the case of what is commonly seen as 'competence-based assessment', however, we are always dealing with a large number of criteria which together make up competence. At this point the issue of compensation and *aggregation* looms far larger.

Most assessment techniques operate with fairly simple aggregation rules of the 50 per cent pass mark or 'must pass each section' kind. In other words, while there may be very complicated decisions being made by the assessor within a given category, there are relatively few at the aggregation level. Competence-based assessment is rather different because the point of 'intermediate' testing is simply to help determine whether or not an overall construct has been displayed – the holistically conceived competence in question. Very often, in practice, this becomes associated with a particular form of criterion-referencing, that of mastery learning, which in turn gets transmuted into a demand for 100 per cent (or very high – about 80 per cent) success rates on an assessment.

Thus, the NVQ approach requires that candidates meet all performance criteria in a given element. Assessors are still, in that situation, having to make quite complex judgements about the adequacy of performance, and to do so in a very non-mechanistic fashion. However, in theory, they are like academic markers in that they do this only at performance criterion level. The performance criteria are then 'added up' to provide element and unit achievement (i.e. achievement of competence) when – and only when – 100 per cent success has been achieved.

This sounds simple enough in principle. In practice, however, it is not what assessors do. Instead they compensate, make allowances, interpret, explain away. The more experienced the assessor, the more they are operating in a familiar field, and the more they have internalized a model of competence (which may or may not be the same as other people's) the more 'active' their judgemental aggregation becomes. Nor is this in any way a practice confined to vocational competency testing in the UK. American teachers operating within the apparently tight constraints of written minimum competency tests will alter pass marks, or the time allowed to complete tasks, because of their judgements about what the tests 'ought' to be demonstrating about candidates (Smith and Shepard 1988).

As we have already noted, people are often unaware of the degree to which they are operating in this way. For example, in the research on workplace assessment which we carried out for the Manpower Services Commission, we used a 'standard task' descriptor for invoice completion derived from industry and very similar to some of the current standards. Industry informants insisted that the criterion for competent performance was 100 per cent accuracy: mistakes might be tolerated in school but not in the workplace. But in fact, when workplace assessors were asked to judge people's actual performance they did allow mistakes, and did apply compensation principles, interpreting performance in the light of the context and other things they knew (or thought they knew) about candidates (Wolf and Silver 1986). In a recent experiment with MA students I gave sample invoices to groups some of whom had accounting and office experience and some of whom did not. Asked to assess the invoices against the relevant standards, the experienced and inexperienced behaved totally differently. The inexperienced failed everyone, because everyone had failed to meet the criterion: the experienced judged many competent (as had their own workplace supervisors). Who was correct?

Wood and colleagues (1989) found similar compensation at work in the clothing industry in their work for MSC on workplace assessment. When compensating, assessors are being quite realistic about the nature of human behaviour, but the point underlines that made at the start about domain specifications – that the search for a perfect template is a wild goose chase.

The important and attractive guiding principle in competence-based assessment is *to clarify what one is assessing and what someone has achieved*, so that, in particular, a qualification actually conveys specific information about what someone is able to do. What this chapter – and this book – would query is the methods by which these goals are often pursued, and the assumptions underlying these methods. In the case of NVQs we have a requirement that every element of a qualification, every performance criterion within an element, and every application of the range to the criteria must be achieved. Otherwise, the argument runs, we will reduce the area over which competence can be inferred and introduce ambiguity into what is being ascribed. The purpose is to avoid assessor error and inconsistency, but in fact, both assessor judgement and the use of 'compensation' remain.

It may be objected that, while this is true, the NVQ approach does limit their effects. There can, obviously, be enormous variations among assessment approaches in the level at which compensation occurs and reporting takes place. This, in turn, affects the *degree* of ambiguity over what reported performance in a domain actually means. In the case of competence-based qualifications under an NVQ rubric, the aim is to make this ambiguity minimal.

However, there are serious theoretical objections to the imposition of a 100 per cent mastery requirement, over and above the issues already raised. A 100 per cent sampling, and an insistence on total achievement mean, as Forrest and Shoesmith (1985) pointed out, that 'your grade is determined by the simplest task in which you fail'. If you stick with this approach, then, given the inevitable fallibility of assessments, *a large number of people are going to be falsely classified because they will fail one or more assignments in which their 'true score' is a pass*. Control for this by allowing compensation, and you are back with the original ambiguity.

Educational parallels

Secondary examinations (not only in the UK but in other European countries) have been criticized over the years for their opaqueness.

What is being said, in effect, is that the compensating principles are so broad, and the criteria used in applying them so unclear, that the resulting information tells us little, apart from a candidate's relative standing. In an attempt to improve upon the situation, a determined attempt was made to produce clear and unambiguous 'grade criteria' for GCE public examinations, taken by 16-year-olds at the end of compulsory schooling. It was ultimately abortive. It is instructive to consider why.

The objective was to make more explicit the 'likely levels of competence and the knowledge that might be expected from those who obtain a particular grade' (Cresswell 1987). At public examination level, one is obviously dealing with 'competences' or 'domains' far broader and more general than the highly restricted US examples with which we began (if rather more constrained than, say, the MCI example discussed earlier). The problems which the development groups encountered, and which led to the abandonment of any strict form of grade criteria, indicate both how near-universal is the direction which any 'criterion-referencing' programme follows, and how insoluble the conflict between aggregation and specificity.

First of all, the attempt to specify domains led, in every subject group, to the further elaboration of sub-domains, sub-sub-domains – and no doubt sub-sub-sub-domains too. There were two (related) reasons for this. The first was the attempt to pin down the ever-elusive comprehensive list of criteria which differentiated levels of performance, and which could somehow never be made long or explicit enough to preclude false ascription – the problem we met in mirror image in discussing test specification. However, related to this (and this is especially significant in the context of broad competencies) was the issue of 'compensation', and the ambiguity this imports into any summary set of grade descriptors.

GCEs (and GCSEs), like degrees, are reported in the form of broad bands. These conflate marks on a number of different papers, skills, tasks, etc. – generally as a result of adding up individual marks, but sometimes as a result of averaging grades on component elements. The problem is that, the minute you do this, and conflate information, you necessarily introduce a degree of ambiguity about the underlying performance.

Cresswell (1987) gives a very clear example of how this happens, using Open University procedures, where scores on two domain

Table 3.5   Hypothetical combination rules for grades

Grade	Domain 1	Domain 2	Grade	Domain 1	Domain 2
A	1	1	D	*1*	*4*
			D	*4*	*1*
B	1	2	D	2	4
B	2	1	D	4	2
B	2	2	D	3	3
C	*1*	*3*	U	3	4
C	*3*	*1*	U	4	3
C	2	3	U	4	4
C	3	2			

Adapted from Cresswell (1987)

profiles are aggregated to give a single grade. As Table 3.5 shows, A is unambiguous, and B fairly easily understood. But under C and D you get combinations of, say, 3 and 1, or 4 and 1 (printed in bold italic). If what gets reported is a C or a D, can we reasonably say that we know what that means? Do a 4 and a 1 translate, in concrete terms, into achievements and 'likely levels of competence' comparable to those specified for a 2 and a 2, or a 2 and a 3? At very detailed levels of reporting, ambiguity may not be important, but at higher levels one is clearly losing anything recognizable as 'precision'. And because people's achievements are, often, like this – because performance is not neatly hierarchical and progressive, the aggregation problem always remains.

The attempt to develop unambiguous grade criteria for GCSE was eventually abandoned, as the teams became aware that it was simply impossible to aggregate under those constraints. Only an extremely long and detailed profile would come close to the level of specificity about achievement which had been envisaged. However, a shift from reporting summary grades to providing such long profiles was not seriously considered by the working groups, and it is worth noting the reasons why.

In part this was because of the implications for the way assessment (and compensation) occurred. If all sub-domains are reported separately, they also have to have a distinct 'mark' or assessment attached to them. There can be no sampling (sampling being, in effect, a process which allows for compensation and inference across domains). This would have been enormously costly, in development and delivery: a point which has also been made forcibly by the examination boards with respect to Key Stage 4 of the English National Curriculum and GCSE (Stobart 1991).

Even more important, however, is the function and use made of these examinations. Public examinations in the UK are crucially important because they determine entrance to institutions which operate under *numerus clausus* and are therefore obliged to rank and select from candidates. (This contrasts with vocational areas where there is no a priori reason to limit the number of properly trained and qualified candidates.) A long list of unaggregated domain reports – reports, moreover, which are seen as, in principle, unamenable to aggregation – are of very little use to them. This is true even if the domain reports are themselves graded, as was always the intention.

In this situation, aggregated grades were seen, quite correctly, as necessary. All the available evidence on employers' use of information indicates a similar lack of interest in detailed profile information, which is not to say that employers in a particular industry are not concerned with the content of the relevant qualifications (see for example Harrison 1983; Goacher 1984). They want to be confident that a qualification has the right content – but not to have to infer this for themselves from a huge list of an individual's attainments! Employers use qualifications and examination results as a simple sifting device and, given the costs of recruitment, hiring, etc. it would be highly unrealistic to expect any changes in this respect.

For similar reasons, there was never any question, in the grade criteria exercise, that many grades were at issue – not just two (pass/fail). In a selection system, a simple pass/fail boundary provides far too little information on which to base decisions. Many competence-based qualifications hit similar problems because they are used for selection, but many others do not because their purpose is to license for practice, or form the core of company-based training. None the less the essential point remains. Because assessors are fallible, and assessees' behaviour somewhat erratic, and because assessment is labour-intensive and costly, any 100 per cent mastery requirement is conceptually flawed.[15]

System parameters

In this chapter, we have raised a number of problems for competence-based assessment, while also arguing that we can reach quite high levels of standardization with decentralized assessment systems of the type which 'competence' demands. The key requirements are exemplars and networks of assessors – plus a good deal of realism about what can be claimed and achieved.

In an earlier section we mentioned the importance of exemplars in this respect. In France, where the syllabi or *référentiels* are customarily expressed in objective terms, teachers see the formal examinations as the carriers of the 'real' syllabus – a position familiar enough to English teachers in the past! Decentralized assessment is no different. The English National Curriculum also aimed at criterion-referencing, with lists of decontextualized Attainment Targets attached to different levels. However, if you take a National Curriculum attainment target, separate it from its example, and give it to a group of teachers, you will find that they assign it to a whole range of different levels. (This has never failed yet, even with greater familiarity with the targets!) Give the teachers the *examples*, and there is no such wide-ranging disagreement. This means that the examples, not the targets, are what really carry the National Curriculum: just as the English population only really found out what a Level 2 standard of reading was when the books to be used were announced.

In GCSE, similarly, in-service training for teachers worked when, and only when, the boards provided annotated examples of coursework for each level. However, it would be extremely unwise to see exemplars as solving all our problems. Different users read the same exemplar differently: you cannot assume that the aspects which you consider 'key' will be the ones which others identify and generalize from.

In spite of the enormous potential importance of examples and exemplars in any criterion-referenced system (indeed, in any assessment system at all), there seems to be very little empirical research on their efficacy in creating common understandings and standards. We do, however, have a large body of results on 'marker reliability'. Research, from Edgeworth's seminal 1890 article onwards, has underlined the fact that some degree of 'error' or variability in the way performances are assigned to different categories is inevitable. Also marker reliability is lower the less the markers concerned form part of a group in constant contact and discussion with each other.

A-level marker reliabilities are quite high (around 0.9; Murphy 1982), although there are variations within subjects. This reflects the degree to which markers are socialized into the assessment model during joint examiners' meetings at which there is discussion of large numbers of different scripts. (Of course, it says nothing about the desirability of the content or the mark scheme.) The Standard Assessment Tasks, administered by teachers to test children's progress in the new English National Curriculum, have proven much less reliable (Pollard *et al.* 1994). As noted previously, some recent results of our own, with tourist guide assessors in different regions – many with a common training and in frequent contact on issues other than actual assessment – yielded rather low reliabilities averaging around 0.5 and 0.6 (see Chapter 4, Table 4.5). Most vocational examining bodies do not release their figures (for obvious reasons), but there is plentiful anecdotal evidence to indicate that this sort of pattern is standard.

One of the most interesting studies in this respect is the one referred to earlier, of Scottish National Certificate modules (Black *et al.* 1989). We have already noted that the supposedly very specific Stock Control modules actually turned out to be very varied in content and standard. Equally interesting, however, were the results for the apparently very vague and 'woolly' communication modules. These in fact turned out to be highly consistent across the group of colleges studied. The reason was that the tutors concerned – in part because of their own uncertainty about how to interpret the criteria – had formed a close network to share ideas and interpretations and so developed common understandings which carried over clearly into their assessment practice.

The finding underlines how important and, potentially, how effective assessor networks are. They are, in fact, the key element in ensuring consistency of judgement. All the major academic examination systems of Europe recognize this: in English GCE and GCSE examinations, for example, it is the examiners' meetings rather than the mark schemes which are the crucial mechanism promoting reliability (Orr and Nuttall 1983). The levels of reliability traditionally secured in civil service and university Finals examinations (Edgeworth 1890) are only possible if one has a tightly knit group with a great deal of ongoing shared experience.

If we are serious about developing national standards, it is not enough for shared norms to grow up within an institution. They are only too likely to be quite different from those evolving down the road. Unfortunately, the more practical and 'authentic' the assessment, the more difficult it becomes to organize shared assessment experience. The problem is partly logistical – how to get assessors together for the time required, with the correct activities under way. But it is also related to the institutional context within which assessment takes place.

There is a depressing footnote to the Scottish study of National Certificate assessors – one which also forms a good preamble to the next chapter. When the researchers visited the same colleges a few years later they found that the networks had broken down. Increased and institutionalized competition between colleges for students meant that management discouraged collaboration and contact: lecturers became possessive and secretive about their materials and techniques. The finding underlines how crucial the institutional context of any assessment system must be and it is to the *implementation* of competence-based assessment, at workplace, classroom, and national levels, that Chapter 4 turns.

4

FROM THEORY
TO IMPLEMENTATION:
EVIDENCE FROM
EDUCATION AND THE
WORKPLACE

The UK is the first country to introduce competence-based assessment as the sole and mandatory approach for a large section of its education and training system. However, the system remains in its infancy. Although 'occupational standards' have been developed for large parts of industry, most National Vocational Qualifications (NVQs) are awarded through special training schemes for the young and the unemployed, and in a few occupations – hairdressing, construction crafts, secretarial, catering, and retail, where they are used largely for shop assistants. Evidence on implementation has to be built up from a patchwork of sources – some anecdotal, some the determinedly optimistic reports of the agencies responsible for promoting and selling the system.

This chapter discusses the major issues that arise in implementing competence-based systems. It looks first at lessons from related systems, in particular those where clear historical and research evidence is available. These include minimum competency testing in academic settings, and experience with competence-related systems outside the NVQ framework, including professional assessment. The second part of the chapter then examines the implementation of the very specific requirements of NVQs (and, in Scotland, SVQs) and the degree to which they overlap with, or differ from, those of competence-based systems in general.

Lessons from other sectors

Until the advent of the NVQ system, the term 'competency' was most often associated with the idea of 'minimum competency', as embodied in a family of minimum competency tests developed in the United States and used largely in primary and secondary schools. These have now been used long enough, and widely enough, for some consistent findings on implementation to emerge: findings which are echoed by experience with minimum competency testing for (American) adults, and by experience in other countries. Research evidence on the use of competency measures in the professions is, in comparison, relatively sparse. However, it provides additional confirmation of many of the problems and dilemmas which have emerged in minimum competency testing. It also underlines the importance of the social context for how 'competency' is *actually* assessed and certificated.

Minimum competency testing

Many proponents of competency-based assessment dislike the term 'minimum competency', because it implies that the standards being set are inherently low. However, any assessment which is a pre-condition for something else involves definition of a minimum: whether it is the examinations which license one to practise as a surgeon, the driving test or the baccalauréat examination which, in France, is the sole formal requirement for entry into higher education.

The term 'minimum competency', however, is generally applied to a more specialized subset of assessments, those in which public or private authorities have specified a level as part of an explicit policy to raise standards. There is no vocational connotation, as there is with competency testing in general; on the contrary, they tend to be specifically educational. Minimum competency tests of this type have been especially common and important in the United States, where anxiety over the quality of public schooling has been growing for several decades, and where there is strong faith in the effectiveness of legal remedies for social problems. State legislatures in particular have been enthusiastic about the potential of 'minimum competency' requirements to raise the achievement of both students and teachers. The types of test used are typically criterion-referenced pencil-and-paper tests of the sort discussed in Chapter 3.

Minimum competency testing for students was at its most popular in the late 1970s, when a majority of American state legislatures became convinced that 'the testing of essential skills and competencies [would] help raise academic standards and increase educational achievement. The idea is that requiring certification of competencies will prevent schools from passing incompetent students through the grades simply on the basis of social promotion' (Haney and Madaus 1978: 463). Most activity was centred on setting minimum requirements for high-school graduation, though in some cases requirements for promotion from class to class were also mandated.

As with other variants of competency testing, the arguments in favour of minimum competency tests were immediately attractive – how, indeed, could one argue against the idea that graduation should mean something, and that students and teachers should have a clear standard to aim for? Very quickly, however, fundamental problems and issues emerged. As Haney and Madaus noted:

> There are three . . . unresolved problems concerning minimum-competency testing programs: the definition of competencies, the specification of minimal competencies, and the testing of minimal competencies.
>
> (Haney and Madaus 1978: 464)

These issues, and especially the first two, have been dealt with at some length previously, but it is worth summarizing American experience because, unlike most of the more vocational contexts in which competency testing currently applies, it involved high-profile general education. Political considerations therefore made themselves apparent very early on.

As Linn *et al.* (1982) have pointed out, standards depend on human judgement and there is no single, perfect method of setting them. Different methods produce different results and so, given the same method, do different, equally 'expert' groups. For example, the Angoff method asks raters to look at test items and estimate what percentage of the target group would respond correctly. How many minimally competent teachers would be able to correct this error of grammar? How many children who have reached 'mastery level' on this component of fourth grade maths would answer this item correctly? The Ebel method, by comparison, asks raters to ascribe each item to a particular category. The alternatives cover the various possible combinations of difficulty and importance. For example, 'essential', 'important–easy', 'acceptable–hard', 'questionable–easy'. Both approaches can be justified in terms of the dimensions of rater judgement they tap, and both, consistently, produce different results in terms of where the minimum competency cutting scores (or pass marks) on tests should be.

In one study (Jaeger *et al.* 1980), groups of teachers, school administrators and registered voters were all asked to set minimum standards, by deciding whether 'every regular high school graduate in North Carolina [should] be able to answer this item correctly'. The differences between the groups were large in reading, and even larger in maths, and would have had huge effects on the number of students who would actually graduate. On reading tests, 21 per cent of school-leavers would have failed on one set of standards, passed on another. In maths, the number of students who would have passed ranged from 53 to 29 per cent. Moreover, all three groups (the teachers, the administrators *and* the voters) recommended standards which were much more severe than those actually used by the state.

Such results are standard and have direct parallels in British experience. As discussed previously (p. 71), research with workplace assessors showed that the standards which they demanded in theory, when asked for definitions, were extremely stringent – and also quite different from those they actually used in practice! (Wolf and Silver 1986). The tendency of judges, expert or lay, to produce very high standards also has important implications for formal 'standards development' of the current English kind. No well-founded remedy has been found, however: certainly not in the context of 'minimum competency' testing. Instead, when faced with very high standards, set on the basis of 'approved' methods, administrators and test constructors tend simply to make amendments on the basis of their own 'professional judgement'.

The gap between the well-founded, clear definitions which

minimum competency testing aspires to, and the reality of test development, is illustrated by one of the most celebrated of US court cases involving education – that of *Debra P. v. Turlington*. As noted above, one of the most important and widespread forms of minimum competency test is the high school 'exit test', whereby obtaining a high-school graduation diploma is made contingent on passing some sort of formal examination (generally in normal US standardized test format). Such minimum competency tests were introduced in response to widespread concern that the high-school diploma awarded by the individual school had come to represent nothing more than the student's willingness to attend classes, more or less regularly, for 12 years.

The 1984 *Debra P. v. Turlington* case was a challenge to the competency examination required statewide in Florida as a condition of high-school graduation. There were significant differences in the success rates of different racial groups and it was argued that this meant the test was violating candidates' civil rights. The court's preliminary decision forbade the state to deny people diplomas on the basis of the test until all students who had started public schooling before desegregation had graduated. That is, they made a decision based not on the validity of the test but on the degree to which opportunities for successful learning had been denied certain students. However, following this, the actual validity of the test came up for scrutiny.

In principle, this should have meant a full inquiry into whether the test really measured minimum competency, with the latter appropriately defined in terms of schools' purposes and teaching practice. In fact, no such thing occurred. What the court actually did was to survey practising teachers and administrators and ask them whether the material in the tests was presented to Florida students. The respondents' replies (to the effect that it was) were accepted by the courts as evidence of the 'instructional validity' (*sic*) of the test.

Chachkin (1989) notes that, in other cases, the courts have similarly confined themselves to looking at whether the skills in minimum competency tests have been taught to students. He regrets that 'the courts refused to make a searching inquiry into the validity of the examination' (1989: 185) but in fact it is extremely unclear how they could have done so. If American educators and measurement specialists have completely failed to resolve the issue of how to define and specify minimum competencies, how can their courts? The latter's circular approach – whereby minimum educational competency is accepted as being whatever has been put in the test by educators – is the only one open to them.

Setting the standards
The standards set for minimum competency tests might appear, in view of the above discussion, simply to be plucked out of the air. In fact, they are the result of a rather more predictable and observable process. They are 'the result of compromise between judgements of what minimums seem plausible to expect and judgements about what proportions of failure seem politically tolerable' (Haney and Madaus 1978: 468).

At any level of the school system, students' achievements vary. American twelfth grade students, coming up towards high-school graduation, vary enormously in their achievement, like their contemporaries in any other system. Graduation is, moreover, seen as something which all students ought to be able to accomplish: it is not a selection mechanism for higher education, for example. A standard which it is feasible for most students to achieve is thus, by definition, bound to be below what most of those same students are attaining at present. It is also the sort of standard on which a minimum competency test is bound to settle. It is congruent with the role the high-school diploma currently plays in US society. It is also congruent with the political impossibility of declaring that most of one's publicly funded schools are failing most of their students. Setting standards for a whole system which only a limited number can achieve is not, in practice, a feasible policy.

The standard setting process has, predictably and universally, led to criticisms of actual minimum competency tests as embarrassingly or ridiculously too easy. One can argue – as we do here – that this sort of cut-off point is inevitable when there is pressure for most candidates to pass and where the nature of the test makes such a result appropriate. That does not alter the fact that the tests do not achieve their original political purpose which was to raise, significantly, what were seen as unacceptably low standards of achievement.

The US experience with minimum competency tests underlines the fact that 'levels', 'standards' and definitions of competency are not fixed absolutes, to be handed down by objective experts.

They inhere in a social context, and it is this which will determine how they actually operate. We may find it acceptable to have high failure rates on selective academic examinations such as A-levels, but what state wants to put trainee doctors through a hugely expensive training and then fail large numbers? What firm wants to adopt a certificated training programme which most of the people it hires cannot pass? Especially given the lack of any consistent, unchallengeable method for setting standards, any minimum competency approach – or any pass–fail competency test – is bound, over time, to be in large part a function of how much failure is tolerable, or, indeed, desired.

Minima or maxima?

As noted above, minimum competency tests in the United States have been criticized consistently for the apparently low standards that they embody. Their critics have also (like many contemporary critics of competency testing in the vocational field) argued that the tests carry another attendant danger, viz. that the minimum level will become the maximum, and that teaching and learning will be narrowly defined by test content.

The most eloquent attack on minimum competency testing has come from Lazarus (1981). He argues that it is impossible to exaggerate the effect of tests on the taught (and learned) curriculum:

> Even more than their teachers, students know that the test is what matters most. 'Are we responsible for this on the test?' is the student's way of asking 'Is this worth my trouble to learn?' When the answer is no, attention is turned off as if by the flick of a switch.
>
> (Lazarus 1981: 78)

Under a minimum competency system, Lazarus argues, 'good' teaching becomes synonymous with getting large numbers of pupils through their tests. This in turn will drive education towards methods reminiscent of operant conditioning. Learning will be cut down into small self-contained chunks on which feedback can be given to students more or less immediately – the most effective way to improve performance on that particular item (though not the way to develop generalizable skills). Anything not directly represented in the tests, Lazarus predicts, will be excluded from the classroom.

It is difficult to judge how far this gloomy prognosis has been borne out. Students in American school systems operating minimum competency tests did, in fact, retain incentives to perform above the minimum. Selection for higher education in particular is based on relative academic performance, as shown by school marks ('Grade Point Average') and marks on standardized tests such as the SAT (Scholastic Aptitude Test).

More generally, however, we do have evidence on the effects of test content on teaching and learning, and they are consistent with common sense and the predictions of the critics (see for example Frederiksen 1984; Madaus 1988). Educational research in general is united in finding that test content has an enormously important effect on curriculum and teaching. Pass rates on ninth grade competency tests in New Jersey, for example, have risen steadily since their introduction in 1982 (Koffler 1985). However, it is not clear how far this reflects general increases in achievement, or 'better targeted' teaching. Madaus and Greaney (1985) note that, under test regimes of this type, 'remediation becomes simply test preparation' and that 'spot remediation', directed solely at specific test items, is widely practised. It is common for the number of pupils who pass a competency test on the second attempt to rise dramatically and for proponents to see this as a sign of the programme's success. Yet Dunbar *et al.* (1991), for example, found that students who were scoring well on mandated tests which had been used in school districts for some years turned in far lower achievement levels on supposedly equivalent (and nationally normed) tests from other test developers. The current enthusiasm in the United States for more complex 'authentic' assessment, which will develop higher-order thinking and problem-solving skills, reflects in part disillusion with the results of the minimum competency movement.

An historical study of the Irish experience with a competency test at the end of elementary schooling (Madaus and Greaney 1985) showed similar backwash on teaching. Between 1943 and 1967, all sixth-grade pupils in Ireland were required to pass an externally set Primary Certificate examination. The justification was of the usual kind. As the minister for education argued, in a speech to the Dáil, May 27 1941:

> Until we have such an examination, the public cannot have any real guarantee that the actual proportion of pupils who

leave the Primary Schools with a satisfactory knowledge of reading, writing and arithmetic, is such as to justify our huge expenditure ... on these schools.

(quoted in Madaus and Greaney 1985: 272)

The tests covered what the Irish Prime Minister called 'the essentials – the 3 Rs' – and included written and mental arithmetic, composition, reading comprehension and grammar; the type of material covered by comparable tests administered in other European countries at this time, either as a basis of a leaving certificate or for secondary selection (as with the English 11+). For our purposes, however, the important aspect of the Irish tests is that the passing standard was identified with an acceptable minimum achievement, which schools were enjoined to provide to everyone, and by which their success was measured.

The result, Madaus and Greaney conclude, was that

the 'minimum' embodied in these ... tests came to be for all intents and purposes the maximum standard. Over a number of years, as teachers became familiar with the ... tests, previous test content came to define the curriculum for sixth grade. Once the level of pupil performance required for a pass was identified, this passing standard tended to become the target that was aimed at in classroom instruction.

(Madaus and Greaney 1985: 277)

Madaus and Greaney point out that, by modern American standards, this minimum-cum-maximum was pitched at a high level. Large numbers – though by no means all – of those sitting did indeed pass it. However, there were other less-desirable effects, not only on teaching but also on school organization.

Because teachers were judged by their students' results, they responded by holding weak pupils back. All pupils in sixth grade were expected to take the tests so the longer one delayed promoting weak pupils out of fifth grade (and encouraged repeating of grades further down the school), the higher the eventual pass rate was likely to be. With luck, many potential failures would leave school before they took (or failed) the test. Pass rates improved over time but, as the authors note, 'improvement in test performance does not necessarily signal a concomitant improvement in basic skills' for the whole school population (1985: 288). In the early years of the examination – before the inspectorate intervened to curb the practice – promotion rates from fifth to sixth grade fell quite precipitously.

The Irish experience underlines that minimum competency tests do not 'self-implement' in the way their creators often expect. They are incorporated into a system in which individual actors have their own incentives and motives, and which operates within a much wider political and social context. Similar conclusions follow from the very detailed research carried out on one of the more recent of the 'minimum competency' tests: the Texas Examination of Current Administrators and Teachers, or the 'Texas teacher test'.

Texas is one of the American states which has mandated requirements to test the competency of practising teachers. The mandate followed a period of national concern over educational standards, compounded by Texas' own low position on state comparisons (using scores on the Scholastic Aptitude Test taken by all aspirants to higher education). The governor wanted to obtain a large pay increase for teachers, because of a campaign pledge, and as part of a campaign to upgrade the quality of teachers. The test was mandated by the state legislature, in response to recurrent news stories about incompetent teachers, and as a way of easing the passage through the state legislature of what was a very expensive educational reform bill. In legislators' view (Shepard and Kreitzer 1987: 24) 'We have to be accountable to our constituents. We are not going to pass this kind of . . . bill if we can't assure them that there aren't teachers who can't spell or read or write.'

In 1986, therefore, all of Texas' teachers and administrators were required to pass a basic literacy test, as a condition of retaining their jobs. The intention was simple – 'give a test and eliminate the few teachers with indefensibly weak communication skills'. The reality was rather different.

Creating and administering the test turned out to be enormously expensive. The test was for all teachers across the state, at primary and secondary level, and in all subjects. This, in itself, ensured that it had to be a 'lowest common denominator test'. At the same time, tough legislative talk and the short development time meant that teachers became extremely apprehensive. As soon as the test specifications became available, 'monumental effort went into preparing' for the test (Shepard and Kreitzer 1987: 25). The University of Texas produced video tapes which were purchased by school districts; the teacher unions developed materials and conducted workshops; regional centres ran review classes. The training, in the view of the researchers observing the policy, certainly affected the pass rates. Equally, it was in content terms *entirely and narrowly focused on the specific content on the test* and also, and substantially, concerned with test-taking techniques, including ways 'to "psych out" the multiple choice test questions' (1987: 26).

Ninety-nine per cent of the teachers who took the test passed. Many of the politicians and civil servants concerned believed that this pass mark was because the test had forced teachers to study, and so pushed standards up. The researchers were less convinced. They pointed out that those who did not pass were, disproportionately, vocational education teachers who were not required to be graduates – games coaches and special needs teachers, teachers who might well be a loss to their institutions, and for whom literacy skills might be less important than other capabilities. Most teachers felt insulted by the actual test: morale was affected and so, the researchers concluded, was the public image of the profession.

In considering competency testing in general, three points stand out. The first, referred to already, is the way in which the political context of the test, not some absolute notion of 'competency', defined the actual standard. There was actually no way in which Texas could create a test which large numbers of its teachers failed, and which led to the dismissal of substantial proportions of the teaching force. As Shepard and Kreitzer (1987: 30) point out: 'Because TECAT (the Texas test) necessarily had to be a lowest common denominator test, the results were poorly matched to original political intentions.' The second is the direct effect of competency 'standards' on learning – the highly narrow, highly focused response of the teachers to the test specifications. The third is the way in which, once test development got under way, any general consideration of what 'minimum literacy' for a teacher might actually mean became secondary. Competence became what the test designers defined it as being, and it was ease of administration, reliability of scoring, and the need for high pass rates which dictated the content far more than any in-depth exploration of the original criterion, the skills needed 'to perform adequately in their jobs'.

Delivering competency testing: lessons from the professions

American commentators on minimum competency have under-lined the problems with setting standards, and with actually testing competencies. Some of the theoretical problems with the latter have been discussed above, but there are also important lessons to be learned from experience with implementation – both in academic settings and in professional training.

Current advocacy of competency-based assessment is, as discussed in Chapter 2, inspired in large part by unease over the sort of influences on curriculum and learning exerted by conventional testing. Certainly assessment is the most powerful single influence on the classroom or training workshop and there is good reason to doubt the validity of much current assessment, and to question the incentives it gives to teachers and students. However, these concerns are not new. Professional bodies in both North America and the UK have tried, regularly, to tie their assessment processes closer to the actual demands of the occupation concerned. Their experiences confirm how social an activity assessment is, and how far, therefore, the assessment systems we are actually able to operate depend on influences other than tests' technical charac-teristics. This has been very evident in US academic testing programmes, where the cost of testing, and the need to have formats which would withstand challenges in the courts on 'technical' grounds, have produced minimum competency tests which are discussed in terms of life-skills, but look overwhelmingly like the traditional multiple-choice, paper-and-pencil batteries which characterize mainstream American education.

Assessment in the US professions demonstrates the force of these same demands. Like many European countries (but unlike the UK), many occupations in the United States require a licence to practise. However, unlike most of Europe, US legal practices and traditions mean that licensing processes, which are, obviously, very impor-tant to people's life-chances, may quite regularly be challenged in court. The possibility of such challenges exerts an enormous influence on test procedures. So does cost: licensing bodies will not normally receive state subsidies, and no profession-based oversight committee will agree to the costs of the tests (which people may take several times) suddenly increasing by amounts which are completely out of line with candidates' historical experiences and expectations.

Many US occupations have 'focussed on outcomes as criteria for quite some time' (Norcini and Shea 1993: 84). Measurement experts from the area of medical licensing, for example, argue that certification processes should 'warrant the competence of the individual practice . . . [and] should warrant that a practitioner has the potential to respond appropriately to a wide range of problems' (Norcini and Shea 1993: 82). They go on to argue that

> outcomes are the ultimate criteria; they provide measures of the consequences of what is actually done in practice . . . To the public, they provide direct evidence that the practitioners are or are not achieving appropriate results . . . Outcomes assessment avoids many of the problems associated with traditional measures of competence because it is a measure of what actually happens in practice. Conventional measures place the professional in an artificial [testing] situation and assess responses to hypothetical questions. Thus they reflect the potential to perform rather than actual performance.
>
> (Norcini and Shea 1993: 84)

These arguments are familiar enough, and reflect the widespread agreement on factors promoting validity which we discussed in Chapter 2. Given this, what strikes the non-American observer is that the resulting test reforms remind one of nothing so much as the mountain giving birth to a mouse . . . It is true that, in medicine, practical examinations are increasingly important, and required of medical schools and other health education programmes. Overall, though, American licensing and relicensing procedures continue to rest overwhelmingly on combinations of demonstrated study time (measured by attendance at approved education and training courses) and conventional psychometric tests of a multiple-choice type. Any resemblance to the 'output-related' systems conceived of by competency advocates is hard to detect.

Some commentators ascribe the continued robust survival of conventional tests to our inability to construct good competency-based instruments (Haney and Madaus 1978; McGaghie 1993; Norcini and Shea 1993) but it has more to do with the social context of testing – including its economic costs – than with technical shortcomings. Even though current procedures have faults which are widely recognized, they will stand up to legal challenge because of their demonstrated reliability – fairness – and because of the ability of test constructors to produce 'validity' coefficients based on relationships between the test and other measures (usually other tests!). The same article by Norcini and Shea (1993) from which we have already quoted also stresses that, 'regardless of exactly how (something) is evaluated, the process must be consistent with *Standards for Educational and Psychological Testing*' (1993: 82). These standards are indeed important to any professional licensing body, for they are the prime reference point for the courts in passing judgement on the legality of any challenged assessment. Their effect, however, is to strengthen and perpetuate the established psychometric processes which produce conventional measures of reliability and validity and so perpetuate established forms of assessment at the cost of movement towards 'outcomes' or competence-based measures. Once again, the social (including the legal) context of assessment proves crucial in understanding actual implementation.

Professional assessment in the United States also offers further evidence on the way in which competence-based techniques are modified by the realities of costs and administrative feasibility. A study of the evolution of 'competency-based' regulations for teacher certification in one US state provides a full account of a typical case (Winter 1982). It dates from a time when competency-based teacher education was seen as a major force for the improvement of American education (see Chapter 1, p. 5).

In the early 1970s, Massachusetts required that teacher certification become performance based. Certification until then had been based on a transcript of studies showing that the candidate had followed certain courses, and spent a certain time in teaching practice. In future, it was to be based on demonstrated levels of performance. The state legislature expressed its optimism about the process: 'Research has indicated that it is possible to judge teacher performance,' they noted. And, 'Already national associations of teachers as well as state groups are developing criteria standards . . . Other groups may be expected to develop knowledge and performance criteria to serve as a basis for certification decisions' (quoted in Winter 1982: 156). So optimistic were the legislators, in fact, that they decreed that changes should be put into practice within one year.

The commission charged with implementation was expected to use observations of teacher classroom behaviour to judge teacher performance and to set up judging teams which included subject specialists, 'educationists', classroom teachers and administrators. However, it faced immediate problems of cost, practicability and development of 'objective and verifiable standards'. Having developed estimates of the costs attendant on performance assessment, it undertook negotiations with the legislature, only to find that the state's financial situation precluded approval of any such level of funding. An amendment postponed the creation of the teams – in effect postponing 'probably forever' the award of teaching certificates on the basis of direct evaluation of performance (Winter 1982: 156).

The commission had found that evaluating teachers in this way was enormously much less straightforward than the legislature had supposed; that in fact, no knowledge enabling judges to do so existed. However, the point to be emphasized here is a more general one. If a procedure is enormously much more expensive than the one it replaces, and if the latter works 'well enough' (in the sense that the relevant institutions function), the theoretical arguments for adoption of the new system will not prove very powerful. Finance stalled the Massachusetts reforms long before the commission's analytical doubts.

In the event, what happened is that, rather than mandating detailed performance tests, Massachusetts decided to license teacher training institutions. The latter were certificated as providing programmes which met the 'performance-based' standard. Their graduates, in turn, would be licensed. The concept of 'time served' also remains. Winter notes that the commission was 'unable to avoid calling on the extent of exposure as a significant criterion in the certification process', and regulations now specify the amount of instruction, the 'length of the practicum', and the detailed areas of knowledge, listed by subject field.

Detailed standards of performance have been transmuted into completion of a 'practicum' based on the general outcomes – this to be inferred from the fact that it is delivered by an approved institution. Winter concludes that the only major outcome of 'the interest in and work on competency based teacher education in Massachusetts' is 'an improved definition of teaching' and argues that this is a 'significant, though implicit, advance'. His conclusion might stand as a judgement on much past and current competency-based assessment but it falls far short of the claims and the ambitions of its advocates.

Assessing your peers: the social dynamics of professional assessment

Professional assessment also provides interesting evidence on the importance of considering the actual process of competence-based assessment in its social context. We noted in the previous section that professional groups are often very aware of the substantive arguments in favour of 'authentic' assessment and, outside the United States, it has generally been relatively easy for them to adopt more practice-based and competence-oriented practices.

In the UK, for example, the legal profession has adopted a one-year 'skills course' as the required final qualification for practising barristers. While this contains a number of written assignments and tests, a large part of the assessment concerns practical skills, such as advocacy, generally tested through simulations. Medical education – notably in some Dutch medical schools – is also moving towards increasing use of competence-oriented assessment, with the development of complex problem-solving scenarios and simulations. In a report for the Employment Department, Eraut and Cole (1993) surveyed practice in 11 British professions, and reported that all but two employed direct observation by a workplace assessor at some point in their assessment procedures. None of these professional groups, however, has evolved or adopted anything like the tightly defined format and requirements of the NVQ system.

Work in the professions has also underlined the social tensions inherent in any direct observation and assessment of competence. The Institute of Education has just completed a longitudinal study of the validity of different forms of assessment (Wolf *et al.* 1994). One of the occupational groups studied was that of health visitors: experienced nurses who do a further one-year training course, university based, and, increasingly, combining professional qualifications with a higher education diploma. They then work independently, monitoring the health and development of young children, and providing advice and assistance especially to 'high risk' families. Courses for health visitors are approved and regulated by the National Boards for Nursing, Midwifery and Health Visiting.

The health visitors have for a number of years been operating with a form of competence-based assessment in which the more academic subject matter is covered in the college-based part of the course but is, in principle, regarded as subordinate in importance to the crucial practical competences. These are taught in fieldwork (during attachment to an experienced health visitor) and assessed during 'supervised practice', when the student works independently, but alongside a mentor who provides day-by-day support and advice. The assessment is carried out by another experienced health visitor, who is not in the same office/practice as the student and her or his mentor, but visits on a regular basis.

In the past, the health visitors had appointed assessors from the same practice as the student. However, this created major tensions. The assessors were also expected to provide advice and guidance – to act as mentors to some degree – and found that there was a huge tension between these roles. The relationship was especially problematic in the occasional cases where there was an unfavourable assessment given, or tensions arose between assessor and student. The fact that they were working in the same place, supposedly collaborating, and that the student was dealing with cases in which the assessor might have a long-term interest, could turn problems into crises. However, these latter situations were rare. It was the general tensions in the role which encouraged the profession to divide it between two different people.

Examples of the competences assessed in health visitors' 'supervised practice' were given in Chapter 3 (Table 3.4, p. 64) as an example of 'broad' competency statements. Some further examples are given here in Table 4.1. We have noted that, at administrative and teaching levels, these are considered the most important part of the course and the student health visitors whom we interviewed for our study certainly agreed with this view. Nonetheless, we found that:

> in *assessment* terms, it was the 'academic' part of the course which attracted the most (and increasing) attention and effort. It was not so much that here some discrimination could be made between students for, while this was the case, the reports and final results were entirely of a pass/fail nature, with no grading or feedback to students and employers about relative performance. More important was that there was constant in-depth effort to clarify marking criteria, with

Table 4.1   Further Health Visitor Competences

---

7   *Health Visiting Practice: 'Services for the Community'*
At the end of Supervised Practice the student should be able to:
(i)   analyse health visiting and related records in the assigned population;
(ii)   analyse health statistics and socio-economic factors relating to the assigned population;
(iii)   identify and review health needs in the assigned population;
(iv)   ascertain and interpret local policies affecting health;
(v)   determine health visiting priorities within the assigned population;
(vi)   carry out surveillance and screening programmes;
(vii)   contribute to work of committees, working groups and case conferences as appropriate;
(viii) formulate and implement formal health education programmes;
(ix)   identify where self-help groups might be appropriate.

11   *Health Visiting Practice: 'Teamwork'*
At the end of Supervised Practice the student should be able to:
(i)   contribute to teamwork in relation to primary health care;
(ii)   establish and maintain professional relationships at all levels;
(iii)   manage work load using skills and resources of others where available and appropriate.

---

double-marking of assignments, use of external examiners, course team discussions about how to develop the assessment procedures next year, etc.

In the practical assessment, short training was given to assessors, but it was generally assumed that the fact that they were experienced professionals meant that they could discern competence in an unproblematic way. In fact, we found that the assessor report forms, once completed, provided no clear distinctions between competent and non-competent students, let alone between those different parts of the overall competency in which a student had or had not reached acceptable levels. Of course, this might mean that they were all highly competent, but it was not clear how the assessor would know!

She usually saw the candidate rather briefly and infrequently, and it was generally agreed by those health visitors whom we interviewed, and who were experienced assessors,

> *that the list of competences was as much a training entitle-*
> *ment as a source of standards.* The major problem was to
> arrange things so that the student, in a limited time, had
> access to all the areas covered. Discovering what standard she
> had reached – so long as it was not massively inadequate –
> was a secondary concern for which there was rarely time or
> opportunity.
>
> (Wolf *et al.* 1994: 113)

Supervised-practice assessors are unable to assess candidates' performance in depth because they simply do not have the resources
to do so. However, this causes very little in the way of overt
problems because, at present, *no one fails their supervised practice*
unless something awful happens. As one senior member of the
profession noted, 'the final examination is really the interview
when you get accepted on to the course' (Personal communication).
This means that there is no real pressure from candidates to change
things, because they do not experience unfairness.

It might seem that the answer to the problem is clear, if costly.
It is, to allow the visiting assessor more time to appraise and assess
what the trainee is actually doing. However, it is not clear how
far this would, in fact, change the nature of the health visitors'
practical assessments. There is another issue here, evident in the
failure of previous attempts to combine assessor and mentor roles:
the reluctance of people working in small groups, with a common
culture, to criticize, let alone 'fail', the colleagues with whom they
work. This reluctance was very evident among the health visitors
in the Institute of Education study just described. Their professional culture is particularly resistant to the idea of judging people
'negatively'. But the problem is a more general one. In a recent
review, Elizabeth Girot looked at the far larger arena of nurse
training as a whole (Girot 1993). She writes that:[16]

> Continuous practical assessments for these programmes
> leading to registration began to be introduced in the UK in
> the late 1970s and were generally hailed ... as being a much
> more valid, reliable and realistic method of assessment ...
> However, now, with the increasing pressures on the role of
> the ward manager, the introduction of supernumerary status
> for learner nurses and shorter clinical placements, it could be
> argued that continuous practical assessment is in great danger

of becoming no assessment at all. The extent to which experienced nurses are able to supervise and give the continued feedback on learners' progress that was considered such a significant improvement on the previous system of assessments is questioned . . .

The Institute report concluded that

> When asked to appraise and judge their peers or fellow work team members, people's responses tend to be highly clustered, with few 'outliers' in either direction – good or bad. This reflects exactly the processes which are required to create effective teams, and which we are increasingly aware are necessary for effective organisations in both the private and public sector. People have to feel that their colleagues and managers are on their side. Unfortunately, there is an inherent tension here with the requirements of training and certification, where what is needed is that problems should be identified and put right, and that people who are not yet competent should not be licensed to practise. Assessors find it much easier to deliver negative judgements when these are mediated by formal examinations, which are not the examiner's sole responsibility. Unfortunately, it is not only the skills displayed in examinations which are important – quite the opposite.
>
> (Wolf *et al.* 1994: 120)

People's reluctance to pass negative judgements on fellow workers – especially if they belong to the same professional or craft group – may be as much of a problem for the quality and integrity of workplace assessment as the opposite threat, viz. that it can be used to exert control and punish 'difficult' or unpopular candidates. The study cited here highlighted the former problem but individuals are often very aware of the second possibility. A recent survey of MA students who were also practising teachers asked them for their views of different approaches to 'practical' assessment in the context of professional studies (Institute of Education 1994). There was an overwhelmingly negative response to the idea of giving immediate supervisors and managers a formal assessment role – reflecting partly doubts that the managers have the information with which to pass informed judgements, but also serious concern about combining line management with control over qualifications which are being used by individuals for career progression.

Overall, the evidence from competence-based assessment in the professions, and especially in the workplace, underlines the dynamic elements in such an approach. Assessment of this type does not take place in a vacuum, but involves interaction between people who bring to it roles, expectations and motives from the rest of their occupational lives. Once again, we would emphasize how important it is to consider competence-based assessments as part of a system and that a failure to do this is likely to undermine their effective implementation. The next section, in which we examine the evidence on implementation of NVQs confirms this view.

Implementing NVQs

As noted above, large-scale implementation of England's National Vocational Qualifications is a relatively recent phenomenon, on which only interim conclusions can be reached. NVQs are, none-theless, the first widespread attempt to introduce fully fledged competence-based assessment throughout a national system of both education and training. As Wigdor and Green note, there is, in most countries, a dramatic gap between the forms of assessment considered most valid and acceptable for vocational assessment, and those most commonly practised.

> The hands-on test is an assessment procedure honored more in the breach than in the observance. Despite the inherent attractiveness of assessing actual performance in a controlled setting, the enormous developmental expense and logistical difficulties of administering hands-on tests has meant that the method has been largely unrealized until now.
>
> (Wigdor and Green 1991: 60)

For this reason alone, any evidence on how implementation of NVQs has proceeded is of quite general interest.

The structure of NVQs is reviewed in some detail in Chapter 1, but a recapitulation of features with key implications for delivery may be helpful. National Vocational Qualifications are based on the 'occupational standards' derived for occupations by 'lead bodies', which represent their industry and are supported by Government funding for this express purpose. NVQs can be at one of five levels,[17] each of which is defined expressly in competence terms, and it is Government policy to encourage the gradual incorporation into the NVQ framework of all vocational awards. This policy has had considerable but far from total success. In publicly funded parts of the education and training system, NVQs can be, and are, demanded. Thus Government training schemes and further education colleges have funding tied to NVQ provision, and adoption of NVQs is also encouraged by Training and Enterprise Councils (which subsidize firms' training) and by provision of funding to professional bodies to develop their own standards.

However, the professions and semi-professions have generally resisted a move to NVQs. In some areas, public funding is largely irrelevant (e.g. banking, accountancy) and the chartered institutions which run the awards therefore perceive little need to cede independence. In others, reluctance to move to NVQs is shown by the key Government departments (e.g. Health, Education) who do not wish to give control to a quango overseen by a rival department (Employment), and who also express genuine reservations about the nature of NVQs. The most important of these reservations concern the extent to which NVQs neglect the teaching of theory and encourage a narrow and atomistic approach to both teaching and assessment. This section discusses whether evidence on NVQ implementation indicates that these reservations are well founded. However, it must be emphasized that this evidence is drawn, to date, from a limited set of occupations and settings.

NVQs are about *occupational* competence, and this is reflected in the definition of the different levels of award (see Table 4.2). The same underlying concept drives the way assessment of an NVQ is conceived. While no particular method of assessment is explicitly precluded, the preference is always for something as close to reality as possible: 'The key is *assessment of performance* ... To achieve an NVQ, an individual must *demonstrate competent performance*' (Fletcher 1991: 26; italics original). Individuals are expected to accumulate evidence of their competence with the assessor expected to bear in mind that 'assessment of performance in the course of normal work offers the most natural form of evidence of competence, and has several advantages, both technical and economic' and that 'performance evidence should feature in the assessments for all elements of an NVQ' (NCVQ 1991: 21).

The other crucial aspect of NVQ assessment is the requirement

Table 4.2   Levels in the NVQ framework

Level 1	Competence in the performance of a range of varied work activities, most of which may be routine and predictable.
Level 2	Competence in a significant range of varied work activities, performed in a variety of contexts. Some of the activities are complex or non-routine, and there is some individual responsibility or autonomy. Collaboration with others, perhaps through membership of a work group or team, may often be a requirement.
Level 3	Competence in a broad range of varied work activities performed in a wide variety of contexts and most of which are complex and non-routine. There is considerable responsibility and autonomy, and control or guidance of others is often required.
Level 4	Competence in a broad range of complex, technical or professional work activities performed in a wide variety of contexts and with a substantial degree of personal responsibility and autonomy. Responsibility for the work of others and the allocation of resources is often present.
Level 5	Competence which involves the application of a significant range of fundamental principles and complex techniques across a wide and often unpredictable variety of contexts. Very substantial personal autonomy and often significant responsibility for the work of others and for the allocation of substantial resources feature strongly, as do personal accountabilities for analysis and diagnosis, design, planning, execution and evaluation.

for exhaustive assessment. Evidence of competence must be provided for each of the 'performance criteria' but also for *everything itemized in the additional 'range statements'*. Range statements 'elaborate the statement of competence by making explicit the contexts to which the elements and performance criteria apply' (NCVQ 1991: 14), and two examples are provided in Table 4.3. This requirement is seen by NCVQ as an essential aspect of competence-based assessment. A competence-based award is a statement about the holder's very specific abilities – a statement that they have mastered all the elements of the competence in question. Without exhaustive assessment, it is argued, no such claim

Table 4.3   Sample range statements

(a) *A publishing range statement: applies to preparation of production estimates*

Production estimates to include following components: editing and proof-reading; typesetting; reproduction of illustrations; materials; printing and binding; reprint factors; current market rates; current production capacities of potential suppliers; technical processes available.

Refinement of estimates includes: from publication-decision stage to final estimates; selling price, print run, and profit and loss per title; global publishing possibilities including freight costs, currency fluctuations, buying forward systems and lead times.

Types of books covered by production estimates include: text only; text with line illustrations; full colour books; heavily illustrated books.

Cost allocation to include: categorization by process; invoicing procedures and interpretation of contents; interpretation of suppliers' scales and cost calculation; costs per page of origination; procedures for achieving page-by-page costings and estimates; manufacturing costs calculations; alternative procedures and costs for producing illustrations; methods of presenting estimates.

Global publishing requirements to include: shipping and freight costs and CIF and FOB procedures; customs clearance and documentation requirements; currency exchange arrangements and forward exchange mechanism.

(b) *A child care range statement: applies to maintaining a reassuring environment for children*

Types of environment: the physical environment; social/personal environment.

Characteristics of children: those from dominant cultural group; those from other cultural groups; those new to the setting; those whose sense of security has been disturbed for other reasons.

---

can be made, and the approach loses its superiority over traditional awards from which no such clear inferences can be drawn.

National Vocational Qualifications now include not only performance criteria, range statements and lists of underpinning knowledge (see Chapter 1), but also detailed sets of assessment requirements. These are now centrally laid down, forming part of the standards. Their introduction formed part of a continuing effort to secure standardization through written formats – something which we have argued was ultimately doomed – and they have been created in a rather curious fashion. Consultants are hired, who may have had nothing to do with the development of the standards, and asked to write the assessment requirements. They do this simply on the basis of the standards themselves which, in theory, are so transparent that this is possible. There is no obligation, during this process, to take any explicit account of time, cost or any other resource constraints.

The following sections examine the evidence of implementation in further education, and in the workplace. They pay particular attention to the issues raised in the first part of this chapter: the effect of the social and political context, the effects on teaching and learning, and the degree to which actual assessment techniques are driven by cost and time constraints rather than the substantive requirements of the competences concerned. First, however, we review the experience of NVQ developers with the actual definition of competence.

Defining 'standards'

In reviewing the evidence from American minimum-competency testing, we noted the uniform tendency of different groups of experts, and different standard-setting procedures, to produce different results. In theory, occupational standards of competence should face fewer problems, because there is a 'standard' out there already, in the form of occupational practice and requirements.

However, this is, at best, something of a convenient fiction. In many industries, there is huge variety in the 'standard' which different firms expect and the creators of the UK standards programme have, in fact, seen the programme as embodying best practice rather than some average of current activity. At the same time, the standards must be 'industry-based', and derive their legitimacy from this.

Competence-based assessment is often contrasted – as is criterion-referencing as a whole – with the stigmatized approach of 'norm-referencing'. However, in practice, the distinction is not so clear. As the evaluators of the experimental US programmes described in Chapter 1 observe:

> The difference between the *degree of attainment* according to some defined standards and the measurement of *relative*

behavior of two or more individuals is meaningful to competence-based programs because it reduces emphasis on the ranking of students and promotes egalitarianism. But it can be argued that the 'defined standards' of criterion-referenced evaluation are derived from a normative consensus of what is required, for example, of a well-trained nurse or teacher; and in this sense, a student's performance is measured in terms of his or her level of attainment 'relative to' the normative standards of a defined population.

(Grant et al. 1979: 147)

We have seen something like this process at work in the way 'minimum competency' standards are set, with different expert groups' ideas about what respondents 'ought' to be able to answer hitting the reality of what proportion 'ought' to be allowed to fail. However, in the context of competency-based assessment, there is generally far more conflict not simply about the level or standard at which competency should be assigned, but about what competency ought to mean. People's norms are likely to differ quite as much as their actual practice – and this becomes more and more apparent the further one gets from traditional crafts whose output is visible and tangible. It is relatively easy to get agreement on what is required for an under-chef in a commercial kitchen to be 'competent'. It is almost impossible to get genuine agreement from all parts of the sector on the competences involved in work in children's nurseries – or being a teacher. Serious differences which relate to fundamental views of society and people, as well as to job demarcations and future trends, inhere in the process, and are not something which can be solved in a technical fashion.

A personal anecdote, drawn from the development of standards for those working with children under 7 years, will illustrate the problem. The author was involved, as a consultant, in a number of experimental workshops intended to improve the ways in which 'underpinning knowledge' was expressed in the standards – in other words, to make it clearer to people using them what theory and background knowledge was required as a part of full 'competence'. The workshops involved groups of experienced practitioners, who were asked to work with standards which had already been drafted, but only to 'performance criterion' level – that is, the outputs or performances had been defined, but there was no list of knowledge, and either limited or no 'range statements' (see Chapter 1 and p. 101 for an explanation of these terms).

One of the elements in the draft standards was entitled 'Develop relationships with parents of young children.' This element had been drafted by the consultant responsible for the standards after consultations, drafts and redrafts, and was just one element among over 100.[18] Its very first performance criterion caused trouble. It read:

2.1.1 Communication with parents makes clear that their presence in the child care setting is welcomed ...

Now, among most contemporary child-care professionals, this is indeed the received wisdom. Parents should be welcomed in, and free to come and go freely. However, there is a very well established, and extremely successful nursery schooling approach, which has no such view: the Montessori method. Here, the classroom is seen as the territory of the child and the teacher, but not of the parent, who comes in only on sufferance, when invited. It is the child and the teacher, and not the parents, who are the experts. There is certainly no evidence to suggest that the Montessori method is necessarily wrong in its approach – on the contrary, it is successful, popular, and founded on well-articulated principles. Yet, as one of the panel pointed out, if the standards were to be taken seriously, one would have to judge any Montessori teacher non-competent.

This particular issue was not one we resolved but it illustrates clearly the type of debate over definitions which runs through the standards development process. So, too, did the results of the workshops as a whole. Two sets ran in parallel, looking at the same elements. The lists of 'underpinning knowledge' they produced differed substantially and substantively yet the make-up of the panels in terms of organizations and occupations represented was very similar. Again, in both sets of workshops, the panel members expressed considerable dissatisfaction with the draft standards they were working with. They made strong recommendations for changes which were passed on to the original consultant group who had drafted the standards. Almost without exception, these recommendations were rejected not on the basis of yet another consultation, but as incompatible with the model which had developed in the course of the original, prolonged drafting process.

This series of events encapsulates, in miniature, the tensions inherent in defining competence for assessment purposes. The English standards programme in effect answered the question, 'Whose standards are they?' by entrusting the bulk of the development work to consultants, who, while they would consult widely, did the major drafting, and thereby steered and moulded the process. As individuals working on these standards essentially full time, they could and did make decisions, and create more or less internally coherent documents, which were then approved or slightly amended by the busy professionals and industry representatives overseeing the process on behalf of their industry body.

In other words, just as minimum competency tests levels in the United States are ultimately defined by the professional test constructors, so competency in the UK is ultimately defined by the professional consultants who write standards. This is a necessary and unavoidable situation – but it cannot create agreement where there is none, and it is a far more active process of standards 'creation' than the official descriptions of standards 'derivation' imply. In fact, one of the advantages of competence-based developments may be the way in which they make public the ultimately arbitrary quality of many decisions about content and standards.

One other feature of the definition process needs emphasizing, because it is so directly related to many of the implementation issues which have arisen. In Chapter 3 we discussed the tendency of criterion-referenced systems of all sorts to get caught in a cycle of never-ending definition and detail, and noted that NVQs had been particularly badly affected. However, the voluminous nature of 'standards' and NVQs is not only a product of the underlying theory of assessment. It also results from the political process of definition – and underlines, once again, the importance of discussing assessment techniques in their social and political context.

In developing standards, although the final drafting is undertaken by consultants, it follows a genuinely time-consuming and wide-ranging consultation process intended to encourage the various parts of the industry to 'own' the standards and, more directly, use them and incorporate NVQs into their training. (Consultation with education is not a core part of the process in the same way. The idea is that these are industry-based – to determine whether they are deliverable in educational institutions has never been part of the consultants' brief.)

The people who are consulted often have strong views about the sorts of competencies and 'behaviours' their particular organizations require, and also feel that, having been asked for some (additional) input, they are honour bound to provide some! The combination of different underlying normative concepts, different activities and priorities in different parts of an industry, and the desire to help tends to produce voluminous amounts of material. The consultant, in turn, does not wish to reject totally anyone's input, and is also under considerable political pressure from the relevant government departments to 'keep the whole industry on board'. Faced with these pressures, his or her response is rational and predictable: put everything possible in.

Thus, the standards grow apace. Range statements, in particular, can be seen as direct indices of how wide the consultation has been. As we shall see below, however, this rationality on the part of those writing the standards – and who are not usually in the business of delivering assessment or training – creates major problems for the education and work-based assessors who are. It is to implementation at these levels that we now turn.

Implementation in further education

Although NVQs were conceived in terms of workplace training and assessment, a very high proportion are in fact delivered in further education colleges (and many of the rest in specialized training institutions for young people and the unemployed). However, no systematic studies of the implementation of NVQs in education have been published. Although a number of publications report on perceptions of competence-based assessment, early planning and preparation, and staff development needs (see for example Burke 1989) there is very little on actual experiences and practice. The early studies do make clear that further education teachers had widely differing interpretations of what competence-based assessment actually meant, and considerable problems with operating a two-category system (pass/fail) rather than one which allowed for more levels (e.g. requires constant supervision/some supervision/operates independently) (Haffenden and Brown 1989).

Later reports by inspectors of the Employment Department on implementation and quality in a number of the more popular lower-level awards have never been made public. Moreover, since the Government's statistics do not indicate where a candidate took their award, it is impossible even to document the numbers involved in competence-based awards in further education. In some occupational sectors they are now the dominant type of qualification, while in others hardly any are offered.

However, college staff have been acutely conscious of the arrival of competence-based approaches even when not directly involved. This is partly because of the heavy publicity given to NVQs, partly because of competition for special projects and grants from the Employment Department, most of which are directly linked to competence-based approaches, and partly because of the requirement that any staff who will be assessing competence-based awards within the NCVQ framework acquire special 'assessor awards'. These latter currently dominate colleges' staff-development programmes.

The major areas in which NVQs have replaced old college-based awards are the craft areas of construction, hairdressing, catering and 'business administration' (basically secretarial). The former are industries where trainees have traditionally been sent to college for their formal training, because the structure of the industries militates against workplace training. In the latter, NVQs have replaced older secretarial training, especially for part-time students, although well-established skill tests (e.g. the RSA typing awards) also co-exist alongside NVQs.

The vast majority of NVQs awarded are at Levels 1 and 2. At technician and business management level, there has been considerable resistance to NVQs, with the older BTEC Diploma awards holding their ground. It seems likely that these diplomas will in fact be incorporated into the more traditionally 'educational' GNVQ (General National Vocational Qualification) system rather than ever becoming fully fledged competence-based awards.

There has also been very little take-up of NVQs being offered in areas with no tradition of college-based craft training (e.g. art and design; computing). Two factors seem to be crucial. One is related to the structure of different industries – their perceived need for specialized training for their workers, and the extent to which they can provide it in-house.[19] Tradition and habit also matter. Overpressed employers (especially in small and medium firms) will generally follow something close to whatever training pattern they were following last year, and the year before, unless faced with very strong reasons not to.

The other important factor is the structure of Youth Training schemes – the most important source of NVQ candidates. Youth Training is offered to any 16- or 17-year-old who is not in employment or education and effectively compulsory for this group since their eligibility for benefit was removed. The craft industries named above were also, for the most part, industries which had powerful training boards.[20] These boards developed their industry's standards, became involved directly in the award of NVQs, and offer and often run training schemes in their area. They are thus in a powerful position to support and promote NVQs (as they are funded to do by the Employment Department). The general view – in the absence of any definite figures – is that most NVQs are awarded to trainees on Youth Training schemes. Many of the latter receive all their training and assessment (on and off the job) within programmes run by independent 'Managing Agents' but many more attend further education colleges for part of their training, or are in schemes for which the local college is the Managing Agent.

The assessment burden
Both this chapter and Chapter 3 have noted the way in which NVQs have generated ever more detailed assessment requirements of a rather atomistic type, to be provided in either authentic workplace environments or the closest possible simulated equivalent. Certainly the perception of staff in further education is that, as a result, they spend a very high proportion of their time on assessment rather than on teaching. Analysis of the requirements of popular NVQs indicates that, if they are to meet the awards' mandatory conditions, they have no choice but to do so and that, in many cases, it is actually impossible to do all the assessments required in the time available.

The author and a colleague looked at the assessment implications of one of the most popular areas, Business Administration, with reference to a seven-module (or seven-unit) Level 2 NVQ designed for delivery in further education (Watson and Wolf 1991). Full-time students would normally be expected to complete this in a single year.

For illustration, we chose the Finance module – total value

1.0 unit (i.e. a seventh of the full diploma). This module was written to involve practical demonstration of 12 'competences' out of a total of 63 for the whole diploma. Each of these competences was in turn structured as an NVQ 'element', involving 'performance criteria', 'range statements', statements of 'underpinning knowledge' which the candidate must also acquire, and detailed assessment guidance. The Finance module competences (elements) were:

1 Make and record petty cash payments.
2 Receive and record payments and issue receipts.
3 Prepare for routine banking transactions.
4 Make payments to suppliers and others.
5 Reconcile incoming invoices for payment.
6 Prepare and despatch quotations, invoices and statements.
7 Process expense claims for payments.
8 Order office goods and services.
9 Process documentation for wages and salaries.
10 Process direct payment of wages and salaries.
11 Arrange credit transfers.
12 Maintain cash book.

We noted that the 'performance criteria' with which all specifications start

> are the bedrock of the NVQ approach. Every one must be met: there is no '50% pass mark'. An excellent principle – except that the finance module alone contains 72 of these performance criteria; and only some can be combined in the same assignment.

The payroll area provided typical examples of performance criterion wording. Remember that these performance criteria are taken from single elements of a single unit and that to this unit or module (with its 72 performance criteria) must be added all the performance criteria for the other six units.

Among the payroll-related performance criteria (numbers 9 and 10 in the above list) were requirements that:

> 'Gross pay is calculated correctly from appropriate documentation'; that statutory and voluntary deductions are calculated using 'standard tables and reference books'; that 'all returns are accurately completed'; discrepancies 'identified and dealt

with'; and pay queries handled. At the very least, any teacher will be faced with a huge problem in preparing materials that involve these separate tasks.

We have described (p. 26, 107) how the 'range statement' appeared in NVQs in an attempt to clarify and further define the standard of the award but also became a way of satisfying all the different interests and suggestions of those involved in the consultation process. The result has been long lists of further assessment requirements, since direct evidence must be provided of candidates' proficiency on all elements of the range. Remaining with this one unit (of a seven-unit award), our analysis noted:

> Following the performance criteria there comes a 'range statement' – and there is a different one for each of the 12 competences in this finance module. This statement is as important as the performance criteria. It shows how far a student's competence must reach – the answer in this case being remarkably far. We find that, in addition to dealing with income tax, National Insurance, pensions, bonuses, overtime, and a whole range of records, students who succeed on this competence must also learn to deal with attachment of earning, SSP, maternity and holiday pay, P60s, P45s, and P46s. And remember this will be one competence among 63.

This example illustrates clearly all the problems of the range statement as carpet-sweeper, piling up everything that has been left lying around. In what sense can a candidate be expected to learn, in the course of a short module, how to deal with areas which tax an experienced payroll clerk – a module only part of which deals with payroll at all, and which demands a large number of time-consuming practical activities? Since the typical candidate for a Level 2 NVQ is a recent school-leaver on a Youth Training scheme, one assumes that they are not expected to reach the level of expertise of a qualified accountant or accounting technician. However, it is not clear, in that case, what sort or level of competence *is* being accredited with respect to this list of 'range' requirements.

The actual content of the NVQs now being delivered, as with more traditional awards, now inheres increasingly in the specific assessment requirements. Taking as our reference point a one-year course delivered in a further education college – a common route for Level 2 Business Administration awards – we wrote:

Finally, we arrive at the specific assessment guidance. Remember, this is one competence among twelve in a single-unit module ... We can allow 4 weeks teaching time for the finance module (as a whole), or about three competences ... per week.

... the documentation expresses a preference for workplace assessment, while laying down strict requirements for simulations. Here, the student needs to operate a payroll of twenty employees on at least four separate occasions and that means not four attempts, but four occasions when he or she gets the entire payroll completely correct. Take a typical further education class of twenty students, two days (if we're generous) to teach and assess all of this ... Elementary arithmetic will defeat the most devoted.

In Chapter 3 we argued that current NVQs are based on a flawed assessment system which strains after unattainable levels of precision in the definition of outcomes. Difficulties have then been compounded by the political pressures which produce hugely inflated range statements. The example above encapsulates the worst sort of result: NVQs which it is simply impossible to implement effectively as they stand.

However, other critics have focused on another aspect of delivery: the degree to which an emphasis on 'skills' has driven out theoretical understanding. By far the most prominent attack was made in a Channel 4 television programme presented by Professor Alan Smithers, and in the report which was published to accompany it (Smithers 1993). Describing the NVQ structure as a 'schematic framework derived from behavioural psychology ruthlessly applied', the report identifies the following points as characteristic of NVQs:

It has been assumed that if students can show themselves capable of carrying out specified tasks, the necessary knowledge and understanding must have been acquired also and need not be separately assessed ... Teachers preparing students for NVQ ... qualifications have been given little or no guidance as to what it is they should actually teach. They have been given no syllabus ... Because the emphasis is on what students can do, rather than on what they know, teachers are discouraged from teaching in a conventional sense ... Similarly, because of the disregard amounting to disdain for 'knowledge', there are no conventional written examinations.

(Smithers 1993: 9)

Many of the aspects of NVQs to which Smithers objects are, of course, features of competence-based approaches generally. They derive their justification from the literature we reviewed in Chapter 2, which suggests that competence-oriented assessments are likely to have far greater validity than more conventional approaches. However, the concerns which Smithers voices about the way in which NVQs have been implemented are shared by a good number of occupational specialists, especially in the craft areas where the new awards have been most fully implemented. For his report, he focused on plumbing and electrical awards, marshalling comments from a number of experienced lecturers and trainers in these fields in support of his arguments.

Smithers notes that, for old-style craft qualifications, there were written assignments and multiple-choice examinations as well as practical simulations. Now

there are no compulsory written tests. Instead there is an attempt to correct what is perceived to be a flaw in ... over-representing theoretical aspects that were never likely to be used day-to-day. ... [However] it is difficult to see how the new NVQs for either plumbers or electricians match the standards of the qualifications now being phased out to make way for them ... There is no requirement for theoretical knowledge to be tested ... [and it] is widely feared among electricians that the new NVQ2 will develop with nothing like the technical knowledge and installation skills provided by the present training scheme ... and that the skills base of electricians in this country will ... be severely eroded.

(Smithers 1993: 23–4)

The major thrust of Smithers' argument is that high-quality training and qualifications are impossible – probably in principle and certainly in practice – unless the assessment techniques used include written examinations concerned with knowledge and theory. This argument has also been advanced consistently by Sig Prais and his colleagues at the National Institute for Social and Economic

Research in London, who emphasize the importance of written examinations in continental European systems (see for example Prais 1993; Mason *et al.* 1992; Steedman and Hawkins 1994).

There is, in fact, no reason in theory why a competence-based system should not include written assessments – why it should not, indeed, be based entirely on them, if appropriate. What does matter is that the assessment techniques should be derived from the nature of the competence, and not be taken as given. This means that there should also be no automatic presumption in favour of practical tests at the expense of written ones – a presumption which, Smithers argues, inheres in the NVQ approach.

It is difficult to evaluate Smithers' conclusions and charges because, as already noted, there is very little empirical evidence available on implementation of NVQs. However, Smithers' argument – that NCVQ pushes practical testing and opposes the use of written tests – reflects a widely shared perception, especially among the craft occupations. A recent survey of candidates' perceptions of NVQs, carried out by Lancaster University, also found that NVQs were seen as oriented towards very specific skills (McHugh *et al.* 1993). On the other hand, the relatively few awards accredited and offered to date at higher levels do retain a much greater emphasis on written tests. (One set of these, the awards of the Association of Accounting Technicians (AAT), is discussed in the next section.)

The one in-depth published study of NVQs in further education relates to construction (Callender 1992). At the time of the research only Level 2 NVQs were being delivered generally, and the report notes that staff considered them to be 'narrow, simplistic, mechanistic ... and assessment driven' (1992: 21). It also noted the greatly increased costs associated with 'authentic' assessment situations – while emphasizing that this is a particularly acute problem in construction.

> Training providers have ... had to make substantial adaptations to their buildings and their use of space. For instance, to allow for the construction of full-sized as opposed to half-sized models, as is required, the NVQ in carpentry necessitates a realistic sized staircase, or the NVQ in brickwork ... work above a single story high ... Many materials are expensive to buy and not re-usable.
>
> (Callender 1992: 15)

The insistence on such equipment derives, of course, from the basic theoretical argument in favour of a competence-based approach: the greater validity and worth of authentic forms of assessment. However, what is also evident here is the danger of creating systems which are driven entirely by analysis of job functions and a quest for maximum validity.

The resulting lack of consideration for costs and time availability can produce unworkable systems in which assessors are, in effect, forced to disregard the formal requirements of an award and assess only what they can afford and have time for. In construction, this may be decided in terms of when the materials (or the money for them) run out; in other areas, by what takes the longest. Moreover, since there is no provision made within an NVQ for regarding assessments as more, or less, essential – everything must be assessed, and everything has equal status – there is no guarantee that what is missed out will be the 'least important'.

Staff are understandably reluctant to admit that they are failing to carry out their formal responsibilities. However, informal questioning of further education staff currently pursuing graduate studies at the author's own institution confirms that staff are constantly making decisions about what assessment tasks are priorities and which can be fudged or even omitted. There can be no formal college policy on this issue, because what is going on is actually forbidden by NVQ requirements. There is thus a danger that a system which is based on theories of how to achieve greater validity will actually produce unpredictable and uncontrollable variation in what is actually delivered.

Related evidence on implementation comes from evaluation of 'Assessment of Prior Learning' (APL) projects. As described in Chapter 2, a guiding principle of the NVQ framework has always been that people should gain credit for displayed competence, however they acquired it. Qualifications should not be tied to training programmes, time spent in education or 'time served' in an apprenticeship, but awarded simply on the basis of evidence of the candidate's competence. APL is the name given to the process by which previously acquired competence can be displayed, and credited. The NCVQ official guidance notes that

> APL gives candidates credit for existing competence. It means candidates need not undertake further training in areas where they are already competent ... NCVQ requires awarding

bodies [i.e. bodies giving NVQs] to provide APL, which particularly benefits adult learners and those without formal training.

(NCVQ 1991: 25)

Considerable financial support has been provided by the Government to help assessment services develop which offer APL to candidates. Some of these have been through direct contracts with colleges, and others through the 'Access to Assessment Initiative' which gave funds to Training and Enterprise Councils (TECs) who in turn used them to encourage APL services – generally, again, in colleges, but also through private trainers. APL candidates are not exempt from any of the general requirements for an NVQ. They have to satisfy all the criteria, provide evidence across the range, etc. Thus, the detailed evaluations which have taken place of APL services provide evidence on the implementation of NVQs more generally.

They confirm that the assessment requirements of NVQs are onerous and extremely time-consuming for candidates and assessors alike (Crowley-Bainton and Wolf 1994). The normal method followed by APL candidates is to create a portfolio of evidence, and to complete checklists showing the assessor which piece of evidence corresponds to which part of the NVQ's requirements – which 'performance criterion', which aspect of the 'range'. The assessors themselves will typically be members of staff at a further education college and their decision will then be checked by an 'external verifier' (also typically drawn from further education).

Often, of course, a candidate cannot provide evidence for a whole award – they may not have covered everything or, more often, simply cannot provide evidence that they have. The process inevitably works better for areas which are paper-based, and in which evidence of competent performance survives in filing cabinets, with the responsible person clearly identifiable. However, even when this is the case – typically for a middle-aged secretarial or administrative worker – the assessment requirements mean that assembling a portfolio is an extremely time-consuming task.

One of the great appeals of a competence-based approach has always been its rejection of 'time-serving', and the opportunity it gives candidates to complete qualifications at their own pace. However, it may be that this very quality is also one of the factors which diverts system designers' attention from the realities of implementation.

A consistent theme of this section has been the impossibility of delivering NVQs as they are meant to be delivered, because of time, space, money, and the realities of individuals' record-keeping capacities. The danger is that, as a consequence, delivery either undermines the quality and credibility of the awards – and the approach – or simply replaces old barriers with new ones. The failure of yesterday becomes today's 'non-completer' instead.

That this is not a new problem, is confirmed by a quote from the evaluations of the early American experiments with which this book began:

> One can ask whether 'time-to-completion' does not become the hidden assessment in most criterion-referenced tests. Probably more than 98 per cent of the nation's twenty-year-olds could satisfy the criterion of changing a flat tire, but those who can't do it in less than an hour are unlikely to be hired by a garage owner, much less by a driver in the Indianapolis 500 who is looking for a helper on his pit crew. Proponents of criterion-referenced assessment would argue that one can admit the existence of a 'pit-crew bias' in the wider society without letting it contaminate educational assessment. Thus [an experimental college] allowed students to 'slow pace' if they wished and placed no limits on the number of trials its students could attempt. But since most of the assessments involved various kinds of laboratory exercises, equipment already put away had to be unpacked for the 'slow-pacers,' and this was often irritating to faculty. As a result, pressures developed over time for students to move along as a group.
>
> (Grant *et al.* 1979: 148)

The US reformers, it would seem, believed they could draw a line between educational practice and the 'wider society'. That, in part, is why their reforms withered. Successful implementation of competence-based assessment, like any other assessment system, required the opposite: that their designers recognize how fully assessment systems are part of a wider social and organizational context.

Implementation in the workplace

More general information is available about NVQ implementation in the workplace than within educational institutions. It was the Government's intention that NVQs should form a major part of general upgrading of training and skill levels in industry, but there is none of the compulsion in industry that applies in public sector education, and policymakers were therefore anxious to discover how far take-up was actually occurring. For the same reason, however, most of the work done has not been concerned with the actual assessment process.

Case studies of implementation carried out for the Employment Department indicate that NVQs are adopted by businesses if, and only if, they can be 'largely implemented with no serious hold-ups to production', and that large companies generally create customized schemes which fit their particular requirements rather than simply adopting the national standards as they stand (Fennell 1992, 1993). Most of the NVQs delivered to date have been highly specific and generally quite low level, with the largest groups coming from big retail chains, where NVQs are used for sales staff training.

The corollary to this is that many smaller companies find it difficult to deliver anything which corresponds to the requirements of an NVQ. The standards for their industry will generally have been developed with reference to large employers, and the chances are small that their own concerns and the way they operate will match the outcomes and range requirements laid down. Frequently it is simply impossible in practical terms for candidates within small firms to cover the whole range of competences, because firms tend to specialize and individuals to specialize even more.

A recent study at the Institute of Education examined the predictive validity of assessments in a number of higher-level occupations (Wolf *et al.* 1994). One of the groups studied was Accounting Technicians, who have developed and approved a complete set of competence-based standards, and are introducing new standards-based qualifications (accredited as NVQs). These qualifications can, in principle, be assessed in the workplace. In practice, college-based simulations remain the rule and the research indicated why anything else is impracticable.

The study focused on the top qualification in the area – a Level 4

Table 4.4 Accounting technicians' areas of work

Area	Percentage for whom this is a central area of work
Cash transactions	26
Credit transactions	15
Payroll accounting	7
Capital expenditure	7
Financial accounts	26
Cost accounting	–
Preparing reports and returns	7
VAT returns	11
Cash management and credit control	7
Accounting systems management	4
Cost analysis and control	4
Budgetary control	19
Appraising activities and projects	7
Preparing financial statements	22
Auditing	33
Taxation	7

Source: Final Report of the Broad Skills Project (Wolf *et al.* 1994)

NVQ award. The standards here are based on careful analysis of the functions of accountants at this level, and on genuinely widespread consultation. Sixteen key functions were identified, over and above those specific to public sector accounting.

When one looks at the jobs being carried out by individuals – the candidates for the awards – and at their likely patterns of work over a number of years, it becomes evident that very few will have *direct* experience of more than a small part of the standards. Table 4.4 shows the results for the technicians in the study sample, i.e. how many were being asked, in their work, to undertake significant amounts of activity in each of the main subsections of the relevant standards. The questions did not extend to whether, within a given area, technicians would have the opportunity to demonstrate workplace competence in all elements, let alone all performance criteria, but merely addressed involvement in the area broadly defined. Even so, only in auditing does the proportion reach a third of the sample, and in over half it is below 10%.

Employers cannot plan their whole production and employment policy around providing experience in all the 'elements' of competence required. Or not if they want to remain in business at all. In many cases, therefore, development of assessment requirements based on an exhaustive analysis of 'competence' results in crippling implementation problems for candidates who are trying to have all their assessment carried out within their workplace.

We referred in the previous section to recent evaluations of APL (Accreditation of Prior Learning) services. In examining workplace delivery of qualifications using APL, the evaluators found that, in the area of Business Administration (secretarial), NVQs delivered in this way were proving attractive to experienced employees (overwhelmingly female) who had no formal qualifications. Because the occupational area is itself paper-based, candidates in this area found it quite feasible to assemble evidence. Similarly, the combination of extensive experience and the degree to which secretarial and administrative jobs require common activities, meant that many candidates could cover the relevant criteria and range.

Other occupational areas had very different experiences. In engineering, 'experienced and competent workers found portfolio collection an off-putting task' (Crowley-Bainton and Wolf 1994: 18). Only a few engineering companies could be persuaded even to attempt APL, and among those who did: 'None of the candidates had realized the "enormity of the evidence" required.' In engineering, 'companies' systems were not organized in such a way as to provide evidence of what had been done in past years' (ibid.). Work by McHugh and her colleagues confirms the difficulties many employers have with APL: 'The general feedback on this route both from gatekeepers responsible for on-the-job training, and also from candidates, is that [APL] is very time-consuming, especially at Level 3 and above' (McHugh *et al.* 1993: 23).

Trying to cover all the required areas could cause serious problems. In particular, there was high drop-out among NVQ candidates in small and medium firms because redeployment and labour turnover (compounded by the effects of recession) made it impossible to cover all the assessment requirements (Crowley-Bainton and Wolf op cit.). Given the relative importance of small and medium enterprises (35% of people in non-governmental employment work in small firms employing fewer than 20 people) current experience casts serious doubt on the feasibility of requiring authentic assessment of all parts of a 'competence' which itself represents practice across a whole sector.

The same study indicated a strong preference among employers for in-house assessment of any NVQs they were using as part of their own training and upgrading strategy. The commonly used alternative was assessment by peripatetic assessors. This preference was phrased in terms of cost, but also of the assessor's expertise. Yet a major area of controversy during the introduction of the NVQ system has been the degree to which workplace assessments can be delivered reliably.

The levels of reliability which are appropriate depend, ultimately, on the use to which NVQs are being put. If they form part of an internal quality system, and are perceived as being tied to companies' own practices, then lower levels of reliability, and general uniformity, are needed than if they form a central part of the training and education system for young people, and are regarded as truly 'national' awards. Many of the problems with the way NVQs have been implemented reflect a failure to distinguish between these two purposes.

The most vocal critics of the whole NVQ regime have been those (like Prais and Smithers) whose main interest is in youth training. Prais, for example, argues that the inherent unreliability of the approach calls for a return to centrally set paper-based testing (Prais 1991). His companions are all with qualifications taken by *Young* people entering the labour market in other European countries. On the other hand the system's designers have also failed to recognize either that there is any problem with reliability, or that the same system is unlikely to serve both 'markets' well. Instead, they have claimed that, in a system where highly specific assessment criteria are specified, and the assessments themselves are authentic, reliability ceases to be an issue. Thus Burke and Jessup argue that:

> Reliability is vital in any norm-referenced system because by definition it is concerned with comparing one individual with another . . . [but in] a criterion-referenced assessment the intention is very different . . . Once external, explicit criteria have been established . . . [there is] an external reference point for assessment. . . . The essential question of validity centres on comparing the judgements made [by the assessors]

... against the criteria ... and *not* between different assessors
or assessments. In these circumstances, reliability is not
an issue.

(Burke and Jessup 1990: 195)

Jessup – currently deputy director of the National Council for
Vocational Qualifications – has gone further (Jessup 1991: 192)
and argued: 'If two assessments are both valid they will naturally
be comparable and thus reliable but this is incidental.' Too much
emphasis on reliability may reduce validity, because one *wants*
assessors to call on *different* sets of evidence, and 'It is difficult to
see in what sense their judgements might be consistent and reliable
in such circumstances' (ibid.). One wants them to be valid 'instead'.

There is a very peculiar definition of reliability implicit in
these arguments.[21] However, this chapter is concerned less with
concepts of reliability than with evidence of how the NVQ system
is actually operating in the workplace. Here, the evidence remains
largely indirect. Previously we referred to two studies carried out
by the author and colleagues. The first of these studies examined
judgements of business and engineering candidates' work by a
sample which combined workplace supervisors and specialist
trainers (Wolf and Silver 1986), and the other examined judgements passed on candidates for tourist guide awards. However, the
first study pre-dated the formal introduction of NVQs (although
the assessment was closely modelled on the emerging format), and
the other involved an occupation in which no NVQ had been
introduced at that time (Clark and Wolf 1991).

The results are nonetheless interesting because they describe
situations which are not likely to have changed very much in the
intervening years, and so are worth recapitulating here. In the first,
trainers were asked to administer a very structured work simulation
task, to do so with candidates who were 'ready for assessment',
and to judge whether or not the students were 'competent' in
the relevant skills. The results demonstrated enormously variable
judgements regarding the level of performance at which a student
should be judged 'competent' even though the assessment criteria
were apparently highly prescriptive.

This was particularly true for the assessors in the business studies
area. However, even among the engineering group, who had recent
experiences with national awards incorporating similar practical

tests, we found considerable differences. Some assessors demanded perfect performance (albeit on a fairly simple exercise) if a student was to be deemed 'competent', while others were satisfied with performances which fell far short of this. The assessors also showed a universal tendency to ignore written instructions in favour of their own or their company's standards and judgements. They did not, it must be emphasized, form part of an assessor network and the new qualifications and modes of assessment were extremely unfamiliar. However, this is likely to remain the case for the bulk of workplace assessment and assessors, especially given the high rate of turnover in jobs which is evident in the English private sector. It therefore seems likely that within-firm reliability and consistency is the best that can be hoped for under the current system, and that at national level large differences are likely.

The second relevant study was carried out five years later in another area, tourism. It involved instructors who were preparing students – many of them adults – for 'Blue Badge Guide' awards. These are held by top-rank tourist guides who provide in-depth commentaries and information, but who are also expected to display practical skills in delivery, organization of tours, etc. The awards are examined on a regional basis, with each region having responsibility for its own tests, but with an active network of 'external examiners' from other regions to ensure consistency, and frequent policy meetings and conferences. Assessors are practising guides, *not* academics or teachers.

As part of the ongoing drive to reform assessment throughout post-compulsory vocational and professional education, the guide organizations had received some money from the Government to help them overhaul their examining system and make their assessments more 'authentic', i.e. more concerned with actual delivery of knowledge in an interesting way and less with factual recall. We worked with them to help them develop some more applied and authentic tests, and then looked at how far the examiners concerned actually applied these assessments in a reliable fashion (Clark and Wolf 1991; Wolf 1994).

The data were collected regionally (because each region's syllabus differs) but for experimental purposes candidates were assessed by far more people than would normally be the case. Normally, assessments would be carried out on the basis of one assessor for the written tests, and two for the practical. For the

Table 4.5   Rank correlation matrices.

Rank correlation matrix for markers (Site A)

	1	2	3	4	5	6	7	8
mark 1	1							
mark 2	.99	1						
mark 3	.70	.74	1					
mark 4	.79	.81	.84	1				
mark 5	.54	.55	.78	.69	1			
mark 6	.62	.63	.85	.71	.93	1		
mark 7	.69	.73	.81	.69	.75	.78	1	
mark 8	.73	.74	.79	.72	.74	.76	.91	1

Rank correlation matrix for markers (Site B) with each other and with candidates' scores on written examination of knowledge recall

	marker 1	marker 2	marker 3	marker 4	exam
marker 1	1				
marker 2	.45	1			
marker 3	.61	.14	1		
marker 4	.48	.58	.80	1	
exam	.17	.15	.23	.16	1

Rank correlation matrix for markers (Site C)

	mark 1	mark 2	mark 3	mark 4	mark 5	mark 6	mark 7	mark 8
mark 1	1							
mark 2	.421	1						
mark 3	.702	.727	1					
mark 4	.636	.452	.755	1				
mark 5	.446	.982	.724	.424	1			
mark 6	.595	.566	.921	.733	.561	1		
mark 7	.634	.489	.738	.929	.475	.738	1	
mark 8	.602	.5	.886	.683	.509	.973	.7	1

Source: Wolf (1994)

purposes of the research, all candidates in a region (typically between 20 and 30 annually) were assessed by all the region's qualified examiners. Table 4.5 presents the intermarker reliabilities for three regions. The results indicate that, even in a situation of established networking and good preparation, intermarker reliabilities on competence-based assessments can be very variable. While some markers show very high levels of agreement, for others rank correlations drop as low as 0.45, 0.23 and even 0.16.

Against these generally discouraging findings, it must be emphasized that, where NVQs *can* be implemented in the work-place with reasonable ease, they often gain high praise from employers and candidates alike. The Lancaster study of candidates' perceptions referred to earlier (p. 120) (McHugh *et al.* 1993) found that favourable comments on the direct work-related benefits of NVQs were common among candidates in employment. While just over half of their overall sample (which included further education and Youth Training-based trainees) expressed overall satisfaction with NVQs, among work-based candidates the proportion was considerably higher. The most common reason was that they had raised standards. As one shop assistant noted:

> On the shop floor I think it did help me work better, think about the job, it does make your standards higher.
>
> (McHugh *et al.* 1993: 35)

Summary

The evidence reviewed in this chapter indicates very clearly that competence-based systems as they are actually implemented are only to a limited extent shaped by the underlying theory of assessment. Political considerations, social dynamics, workplace organization, cost, and the previous experiences and ideas of individual assessors all play as important a role. The more systems are based on extremely demanding and rigid requirements – as has happened with NVQs – the more likely it becomes that factors which are technically extraneous to assessment will in fact preclude effective and high-quality assessment from taking place. Assessment requirements may have a powerful effect on the classroom but no system of assessment and qualifications can, on its own, alter and restructure a labour market, or change the way people behave together.

If the system is fundamentally at odds with these, it is the assessment system, and the quality of its judgements, which will suffer.

Many of the issues and problems we have identified in this chapter will arise in any competence-based system – but not all, and only in varying degrees. All assessment systems, after all, have major problems in implementation as well as in more technical areas. The arguments for a competence-based approach, which we reviewed in Chapter 2, do not lose their force because implementation is difficult, or because unrealistic demands are made of assessors. Equally, these arguments alone cannot justify introducing and promoting a competence-based approach, no matter where and when. In the Conclusion (Chapter 5), therefore, we review the ability of competence-based assessment to meet the demands made of contemporary education and training and briefly map out some possible future developments.

5

CONCLUSION: A LOOK TO THE FUTURE

As recently as 1989, John Burke could write that 'a quiet revolution is occurring in Vocational Education and Training. "Quiet" because the depth and breadth of change has hardly been noticed ...' (Burke 1989:1) Now, this is no longer true. The competence-based system he was discussing is one on which virtually everyone in English secondary and post-secondary education has very strong views indeed, and the subject of newspaper editorials and television polemics. It does, however, retain the characteristics of a revolution. It divides people into opposing camps: those who are not for you are against you.

The proponents number among them many of the Employment Department officials responsible for developing occupational standards. Quite contrary to the usual conception of neutral and cynical civil servants, many of them have become enthusiastic true believers, seeing themselves as shock-troops or change agents in the cause of better training and education. A full competence-based system, they believe, could ensure that 'all formal learning ... would be more effective', give individuals the opportunity to realize their potential, and enable the country to 'make much more effective use of its human resources' (Jessup 1991: 6, 131). On the other side, opponents such as Alan Smithers or Sig Prais in England, or David Penington in Australia, consider the approach to be a catastrophe, further weakening an already inadequate system. 'NCVQ seems to be perpetrating a disaster of epic proportions' is Smithers' judgement (Smithers 1993: 41). Penington argues that the 'competency crusade' is designed to put all education under the direct control of government, industry and the unions, and that it not only 'sells short the process of education at every level but will end up holding back the development of the country' (Penington 1992: 12).

These seem extreme positions. We are, after all, only discussing an assessment method here and one whose fundamental principles do not sound, at first acquaintance, very controversial. As summarized in Chapter 1, these involve the definition of outcomes, the rejection of grading, and the treatment of assessment as a separate self-contained activity, distinct from teaching and learning. Further elaborated by NCVQ, they form an 'assessment methodology' whose opaqueness suggests arcane technical debate, of no great interest to anyone other than assessment specialists.

In fact, however, competence-based assessment does embody a revolutionary position. It is based on rejection of, and antagonism to, one of the huge industries of our time: organized education. Lengthy debates about range statements or evidence indicators are secondary to two fundamental claims: that current education and training is fundamentally inadequate *and* that a better alternative is available.

Throughout, we have argued that the first of these statements is well founded, but the second, unfortunately, far less so. The problem with competence-based assessment is similar to that with many revolutionary movements – the critique has enormous power, but the new order turns out to have as many or more problems than the old. Here, we will suggest that, for both reasons, we have probably reached the high-water mark of enthusiasm for the approach – but that it is likely to be with us for many years to come.

The critique

The fundamental argument against mainstream educational assessment is that it does not measure what it should. As we saw in

Chapter 2, the received view among experts is that assessments are more valid – better measures of what they purport to be about – the closer they are to the behaviour in which one is interested. If you are trying to predict whether people will be good at higher levels of academic study, academic tests are therefore appropriate. Conversely, if you are interested in vocational or professional work, or in practical skills, then they are almost certainly *inappropriate*.

The evidence summarized in Chapter 2 strongly confirmed the limitations of academic assessments as predictors of later performance. It also showed that assessments which mirror closely the activities and environment of a workplace are good predictors of workplace success.

In discussing this evidence, we concentrated on the support it provided for competence-based assessment but of course the implications go further than this. They are just as important for the way we teach and train people, as for how we assess their skills. Michael Dixon has argued strongly that we need to

> clarify the difference between two broad kinds of knowledge. One is the academic sort forming the main stock in trade of ... education ... The other is the type essential to the doing of almost all skilled work ... The academic sort consists of ... quasi-factual knowledge: knowing *that* something is so [and] scientific-style explanations ... knowing *why* they are so. But work skills are based on know-*how*, which is more complex.
>
> (Dixon 1993b)

Dixon's point is that knowing that, or why, is no guarantee whatsoever that one will know how to do something when the need arises. He notes that

> The distinction is hardly a new discovery. Aristotle pointed it out some 2300 years ago. He wrote that absorbing knowledge intellectually is not enough to make it usable. To become readily convertible into skilful action, it 'must be worked into the living texture of the mind'. And while he didn't specifically say so, the inference is that the only way to gain such skills is by diligent practice in conditions that are increasingly real.
>
> (Dixon 1993a)

Dixon's interest here is not in assessment but in the content and style of education. He considers higher education to have been enormously over-expanded, and apprenticeship-style learning unduly neglected. The arguments are, however, parallels of those discussed for assessment *per se*. However, as we pointed out in Chapter 2, and as Dixon admits in his discussion, academic education in specialized institutions, and academic styles of teaching and assessment, flourish in large part because they are cheap and easy to deliver. Formal education and formal educational qualifications have burgeoned worldwide, and show no sign, as yet, of any reverse. Fewer and fewer pupils enter work at the minimum school-leaving age. More and more enter higher education – and parental and student aspirations signal further huge increases in demand.

This means that the institutions and practices which the competence-based movement attacks are not some hot-house plant, promoted and nurtured by special legislation or recent Government support. They are the product of powerful pressures and forces common to all contemporary societies, they serve important functions in the organization of those societies (especially selection and labour market allocation) and they also employ huge numbers of people who will defend their own sectional interests. This in itself suggests that the success of competence-based assessment will have as much or more to do with implementation issues, and ease of delivery, as with arguments from first principles.

Unfortunately, this is not how most advocates have approached the task of introducing competence-based practices. Instead, their ambitions have, from the start, been enormous: to create a revolution, to transform the nature of training and education. As discussed in Chapter 3, they have tended enormously to overstate the capacity of the approach to solve enduring problems of any assessment system – its ultimate reliance on holistic and imperfect assessor judgements. Exaggerated claims, unfortunately, backfire in the end because when a technique fails to deliver what it promised, there is a tendency to reject it wholesale. Misplaced theories about what could be achieved have also carried the creators of the NVQ system, like their American predecessors, down a never-ending spiral of specification. This has created enormous resentment among practitioners, and has rapidly diminishing returns in terms of either reliability or validity of judgement. It may be that faith of this sort is as necessary to assessment reformers as to any other revolutionary sect. However, the precedents are not encouraging. Revolutionary sects have a tendency to wither and die. Only a very few become institutionalized and successful.

The evidence discussed in Chapter 4 is not very encouraging with respect to this particular sect's transformation from a Government-sponsored experiment into the long-term, mainstream approach of vocational education and training. Instead, the findings confirm the crucial importance of viewing assessment practices in their organizational, economic and political contexts. They suggest that, if competence-based assessment is to continue in the long term, it will have to be substantially modified.

Implementation issues

A curious aspect of competence-based reform, at least in England and Wales, is that, although the reformers' ambitions are very wide, their focus has been very narrow. They would like to see major changes in the whole institutional context of vocational training and education but they have themselves treated the approach as essentially a technical affair. The NVQ development process, and the volume of guidance which has appeared on standards development, are almost entirely concerned with assessment as a technical issue – with the actual process of defining outcomes, clarifying the nature of the competence, and with the actual assessment judgement. 'Implementation' discussions are about piloting, training assessors, keeping records of the assessment results, not about how the whole process does (or does not) fit into the delivering organization. Just as, in NVQ 'methodology' one jumps from occupational standards directly to judgements of competence, so, in the development process, one moves directly from a basic rationale to the minutiae of an individual assessment.

In the process, as Chapter 4 indicates, three crucial considerations get overlooked. The first is that a system of competence-based assessment must be delivered by organizations which have their own pre-existing and enduring concerns. The second is that it must be delivered by people who also have pre-existing beliefs, values and objectives. The third is that competence-based assessment is as subject to cost constraints as any other activity. In the long term, people will only carry it out if the benefits they perceive outweigh the costs. These three factors explain the problems in implementation which are becoming increasingly evident. They also suggest where competence-based assessment is most likely to survive and prosper, and where it will probably disappear.

At the organizational level, competence-based assessment systems face a fundamental dilemma. The closer one gets to workplace reality, the lower assessment falls in the organization's priorities. Full-time educational institutions can, and will, arrange themselves around the assessment 'function', because turning out people with qualifications is what they are about. The 'function' of a bank, or an engineering company, is not to assess and qualify people, and there are, correspondingly, very tight limits on how far either the organization of the enterprise, or the time commitments of its employees, will be altered to meet the requirements of an assessment system.

If one tries to introduce into such organizations a system which requires people to perform a wide range of tasks in which they would not normally be involved, it is the assessment system which will crumble, not the organization's work patterns. This is why, as discussed in Chapter 4, small firms, in particular, find full-scale workplace assessment so problematic. Broadly-conceived competences which look at the overall functions of an occupation, rather than at what a given individual does, will necessarily create implementation problems. If, as in England, one then adds to this both detailed 'range statements' and requirements for 100 per cent assessment, the net result will be that organizations simply cannot and will not deliver. Competence-based assessment becomes, instead, concentrated in the very full-time institutions it was meant to bypass, with all the resulting loss of authenticity.

Competence-based systems are, of course, far from alone in the second major source of implementation problems: people. The insistence of people on behaving in ways commensurate with their own priorities and interests, rather than those of the organization, is hardly new. Nor, unfortunately, is the failure of assessment designers to recognize it. The problems encountered by English National Curriculum assessment in primary schools (Pollard *et al.* 1994) also relate in large part to a complete failure to take account of teachers' pre-existing values, priorities and judgements.

Certainly the competence-based assessor of the literature is a strangely bloodless creature, responding purely to the requirements of the standards on the one hand, and the observed behaviour of the candidate on the other. And if by any chance anything does go wrong, then the assumption is that the 'verifiers' – internal and external to the organization – will detect it. Whether or not the assessors will actually listen to the verifiers, or the verifiers feel able to highlight problems, is not something which seems ever to have been raised as an issue.

In fact, as we discussed in Chapter 4, assessors and candidates alike are part of social and workplace groups which have their own imperatives, such as the need to get on well and work together. There is an inherent tension here. The person who is in theory best able to judge a candidate's performance may be the least well placed to do so effectively. The assessment does not take part in a vacuum, but within a social context.

The experience of professional groups which have practised forms of competence- and workplace-based assessment for some years suggests that, in this situation, 'objective', standardized judgements are difficult to obtain. The costs to the individuals and to the group of questioning a candidate's competence will generally outweigh any doubts the assessor may harbour. While occupations will vary in the strength of these pressures, the evidence underlines, again, the importance of viewing competence-based assessment in its social context, not simply as a technical approach.

Cost is the third implementation issue with very clear implications for the future. The competence-based assessment literature pays lip-service to the importance of cost and 'cost-effectiveness', and, in the UK at least, a number of senior Employment Department officials perceive it as a genuine problem for NVQ take-up. However, when one looks at the way the development process has been driven, cost never appears as a central, let alone a deciding, issue. At every point, as discussed in Chapters 1 and 4, it is the 'technical' requirement of greater clarity, or the insistence on 100 per cent assessment, which have dominated.

The result is a system of assessment which is extremely expensive. It is time-consuming in absolute terms, for both candidate and assessor and it imposes major costs in terms of equipment, provision of wide-ranging assessment situations, and repeated evidence of mastery. These costs are not, on the whole, borne fully by candidates or employers – many NVQs are taken through training schemes or in further education, and a large part of NVQ delivery in the workplace is subsidized directly through various government programmes. Even so, in the short-, let alone the long-term, 'cost-benefit' calculations can look very unattractive.

Costs and the future of competence-based assessment

People cannot engage in detailed, accurate calculations of exactly what a qualification is worth to them, but they can and do engage in approximations of just this sort. Their conclusions will ultimately decide the future of competence-based assessment. Of course, the amount of subsidy which the Government provides will alter the equation and make activities attractive which would otherwise not be undertaken. However, conclusions about the *relative* prospects in different sectors stand.

The key factor determining whether a qualification is attractive to an individual is the extent to which it will increase their work and career prospects. (This is not to deny that people study from other motives too, but this is the most important one, and certainly the dominant reason for pursuing a *vocational* award.) Thus a major reason for low take-up of vocational qualifications in England during the 1970s and 1980s was their failure to deliver much in the way of increased earnings (Bennett *et al.* 1992). On the employer side, a similar calculation takes place. Whether employers pay for training or subsidize employees to study, will depend on whether this is seen as worthwhile in terms of directly increased productivity, or retaining and motivating the workforce.

Perceptions about whether qualifications 'pay for themselves' can and will change. For example, current shifts in the structure of the labour market mean that unskilled jobs are vanishing. This will affect the perceived returns to training and study (and is probably an important factor in the recent very rapid increase in the proportions of English teenagers remaining in school). Employers' perceptions may change too, in the light of both expected levels of competition and technical change, and a realization that firms with a strong training culture tend to retain their workers rather than have them 'poached' by competitors. However, this does not alter the fact that perceived benefits have to be set against expected costs. People will only pay for expensive training, or an expensive qualification, if the benefits are also expected to be great.

Competence-based assessment is expensive. This is not simply because of the volume of assessment imposed by current NVQ requirements. It is also because the heart of competence-based assessment is its insistence on authenticity, or face validity – a close correspondence between the assessment situation and the situation in which the candidate will one day operate. In almost any comparison imaginable, such assessments cost more than a conventional pen-and-paper test. This will be true even if – when? – current requirements for 'evidence across the range' disappear. And it means that competence-based techniques are likely to be adopted and survive in direct proportion to whether or not the potential pay-off to candidate and/or employer are also great.

Discussions of competence-based assessment often start with the example of the driving test. In fact, this is a rather atypical example. First of all, it is an area of competence in which a very large proportion of the population has a major interest, and where the benefits of holding a licence are very clear and very wide-ranging indeed. Second, training is delivered by highly specialized instructors and assessment carried out by full-time examiners. Third, and most important for our argument, there is no need to create a special environment for assessment purposes. Even though the examiners are professionals, a completely authentic assessment environment is available to them for free. They only need to turn the car out onto the road.

In terms of lessons for a national system, the training and assessment of pilots provides a far better example of competence-based assessment. This is a case where the industry has accepted completely the greater value of a competence-based, or authentic, approach to assessment. It has also spent large amounts of money creating simulated environments for training and assessment. It has done so because so much rides on success – because the returns to good assessment are so high and the returns to bad ones so catastrophic. A flight simulator costs a great deal to build but compared to the price of a crashed airliner (with or without passengers), the sum is trivial.

As a general rule, competence-based assessment is more likely to be adopted and to survive the closer one gets to the situation of an airline pilot. If the skills involved are uncommon, and command a high return in the market place, individuals will be prepared to pay for more expensive assessment. If the importance of having well-trained, properly accredited employees is high, then employers will feel the same. Which brings us to the conclusion that the occupations in which competence-based approaches are most likely to flourish are those which were closest to them already, before current reforms began: the old crafts and the professions.

Competence and the professions

Current discussions of NVQs and their implementation problems often arrive at the conclusion that 'the problem' is that NVQs started with low-level qualifications. In a sense this is correct: it was easier to believe that one could deliver transparent, highly specific standards for a kitchen assistant than for an accountant or manager. It does not, however, follow, that competence-based assessment is suitable for low-level manual jobs and unsuitable for the professions. In many ways the opposite is true.

If it is very expensive to assess people for jobs which are quite quick to learn, where many people have the relevant skills and/or where differing degrees of competence are quite acceptable, then, without enormous subsidies, the assessments will not take place. In the professions, however, rewards are high and employers (or partners) very keen on at least a minimum guaranteed competence. As discussed in Chapter 4, a number of professions have, over the years, developed competence-style assessments, albeit outside any formal NVQ-type framework, and in a rather *ad hoc*, partial way. In the future, we would suggest, it is the professions which are most likely to continue with this approach.

Direct confirmation of the underlying relationship between occupational structure and assessment style comes from Australia. Gonczi describes how, 'Under encouragement from the Commonwealth government, almost all the professions have developed competency-based standards and are currently developing competency based assessment strategies' (Gonczi 1994: 27). Far from lagging behind other sectors, the professions have actually proceeded furthest and fastest in the direction of competency-based systems.

There are two major reasons for the difference between Australia and the UK. The first is that, although Australian standards have a similar overall structure (units, elements, performance criteria) the professions in Australia operate within a far less restrictive framework regarding the nature and focus of the competency descriptors. The latter are holistic, expressed in everyday language, rather than attempting total transparency at a micro-level, and are tied to overt specifications of curriculum, not purely to 'outcomes'. Second, the Australian professions have an additional incentive to develop competency-based assessments. Australia is still largely a country of immigrants, many of them with professional qualifications from other systems. Knowing whether an immigrant really has the competence to practise a profession is therefore a pressing concern and it is under the auspices of the National Office of Overseas Skills Recognition that much of the development has taken place. Both of these factors, however, are, in the long term, less important than the underlying relationship between the costs and benefits of expensive competence-based systems.

The other area in which we would expect competence-based assessment to have a long-term future is that of the traditional crafts. Here, too, one has identifiable, and relatively scarce skills which are, in Dixon's words, of the 'know-how' variety. One has employers who want these properly certificated, significant financial returns and, crucially, the critical mass required – enough people to justify the expensive development processes as well as the costs of a particular assessment. Incentives (or pressures) to maintain a competence-oriented approach provide a valuable counterweight to the strong pressures which drive assessment – craft or professional – in an academic, paper-based direction.

In other sectors, however, we are likely to find that a strong emphasis on competence-based awards survives only as long as the Government's enthusiasm and large-scale funding. Problems of implementation, especially within the demanding and rigid constraints erected for NVQs, are likely to outweigh the advantages for employers. For individuals, especially the young, more general qualifications and training will offer greater rewards and flexibility than will a highly specific competence-based award.

We have therefore probably reached a high-water mark of activity and enthusiasm for competence-based awards. The process has, moreover, left educational institutions still standing and largely intact. However, the ideas on which competence-based assessment is founded are unlikely to disappear. Its critique of educational awards remained unanswered, and will become more powerful, not less, as educational expenditures continue to rise. And if the basic principle of deriving assessments directly from the 'criterion behaviour' comes to be honoured less in the breach, and more in the observance, then some of the movement's promise may survive its current excessive ambitions.

NOTES

1 Adapted from G. Grant *et al.* (1975) *On Competence: A Critical Analysis of Competence-Based Reforms in Higher Education*, p. 5. San Francisco: Jossey-Bass.

2 Another well-documented response to this call was the 'voucher' experiment, designed to give parents the ability to select schools, and channel funds to the schools of their choice. Only one school district (lea) actually agreed to participate in a modified version of this scheme, which was wound down when large-scale federal funding ceased.

3 Comparable objectives produced 'minimum competency' require-ments for high-school graduation – this time without direct federal involvement. See Chapter 4.

4 NEDO (National Economic Development Organization) and the MSC (Manpower Services Commission) – both now abolished although the MSC's functions have been incorporated into the Employment Department.

5 European comparisons show that England and Wales now produce relatively high proportions of qualified technicians, but have relatively low levels of craft qualification.

6 Managers of Youth Training schemes would often complain about the perceived lack of responsiveness of further education to their

requirements, and forecast that the sector would shrink in the future as better, more relevant training programmes were established elsewhere. While many Youth Training schemes do indeed now provide all their own training, the further education sector as a whole has in fact grown enormously in the last ten years.

7 General Certificate of Education: offered at Ordinary (O) level mostly to 16-year-olds, and at Advanced (A) level. O-levels have been superseded, within England and Wales, by the GCSE (General Certificate of Secondary Education) but continue to be taken by overseas students.

8 For example, in England, law students challenged the results of the Inns of Court skills assessment and the absence of any review procedure for the German Abitur has also been challenged.

9 The huge scale of recruitment and training for the US Armed Forces means that cost and administrative constraints preclude the wholesale use of performance measures. The research described by Wigdor and Green was an enormous research programme designed to validate and improve the (pen-and-paper) Vocational Aptitude battery which will remain, for the foreseeable future, the single most important instrument for initial screening.

10 See Brown (1988) for a discussion of similar processes in the development of the English National Curriculum.

11 Hambleton and Rogers (1991: 8).

12 This is particularly easy to illustrate with mathematics: the Assessment of Performance surveys in England and Wales provide a wealth of examples in which the 'same' sum (even something as simple as three divided into seven) proved enormously much easier or harder according to the way it was presented (APU 1980, 1981).

13 It is for this reason that English examination boards do not decide the 'grade boundary' marks (e.g. at what point the cut-off between an A and a B lies) in advance of administering the examination. See below for a further discussion of this issue.

14 Moreover, to the degree that it really includes judgements about whether, for example, 'work methods and activities optimise the use of available material, capital and people' the judgement will not and cannot relate to 'output' measures. It must, instead, relate to theories about process and procedure which have no place in the printed standards, and have been acquired by the assessor independently of their involvement with competence-based assessment. How, after all, would one ever know that something had been optimized, or used to 'best effect'?

15 We do not have any detailed information on how far the NVQ requirements are actually being observed, and how far, in practice,

assessors are applying compensation across elements or even units of an award. Output-related funding, whereby trainers get more money if trainees actually achieve an NVQ, certainly gives plenty of incentives for creative compensation. However, we do know, from US experience, that insisting on 100 per cent requirements very quickly turns competence into minimum competence. Assessment systems do not exist in a vacuum. See Chapter 4 for further discussion of 'minimum competency testing'.

16 E. A. Girot (1993) Assessment of competence in clinical practice – a review of the literature. *Nurse Education Today* 13: 85–90.

17 Whether higher levels should all be treated as 'Level 5', or whether the hierarchy should extend on into Levels 6, 7 and beyond has been under discussion for years without clear resolution.

18 The standards have been subject to further redrafting since then, and used in a variety of combinations, making up different possible qualifications.

19 For example, construction, which is increasingly made up of small subcontractors, is not in a position to offer much workplace-based training. Catering is an industry where the workplace is under extreme time and space pressures, and, again, unable to offer much workplace *training*, as opposed to experience.

20 Training boards, which were supported via a compulsory levy, were abolished in the 1980s (with the exception of construction). However most, either as boards, or, later, as reconstituted training organizations, became either a major part of, or commensurate with, their industry's lead body.

21 Validity requires and subsumes reliability, even if the reverse is not true. Most people are interested in assessments from which they can *generalize* to candidates' future behaviour and for that high levels of both validity and reliability are important.

REFERENCES

Andrews, T. E. (1972) *The Manchester Interview: Competency-Based Teacher Education/Certification*. Washington DC: American Association of Colleges for Teacher Education.

APU (1980, 1981, 1982) *Mathematical Development Survey*. Numbers 1, 2, and 3. London: HMSO.

Asher, J. J. and Sciarrino, J. A. (1974) Realistic work sample tests: a review. *Personnel Psychology* 27: 519–33.

Bennett, R., Glennerster, H. and Nevison, D. (1992) Investing in skill: to stay on or not to stay on. *Oxford Review of Economic Policy* 8(2).

Berk, R. A. (ed.) (1984) *A Guide to Criterion-Referenced Test Construction*. Baltimore: Johns Hopkins University Press.

Black, J. H., Hall, J., Martin, S. and Yates, J. (1989) *The Quality of Assessments: Case-studies in the National Certificate*. Edinburgh: Scottish Council for Research in Education.

Blinkhorn, S. F. and Johnson, C. E. (1990) The insignificance of personality testing. *Nature* 348: 671–2.

Bourdieu, P. and Boltanski, L. (1981) The educational system and the economy: titles and jobs (trans. R. Nice). In Lemert, C. (ed.) *French Sociology: Rupture & Renewal since 1968*. New York: Columbia University Press.

Bourdieu, P. and Passeron, J. C. (1979) *The Inheritors* (trans. R. Nice). Chicago: University of Chicago Press.

Brehmer, M. (1989) Grading as a quasi-rational judgement process. In Lowyck, J. and Clark, C. (eds) *Teacher Thinking and Professional Action*. Leuven: Leuven University Press.

Brown, M. (1988) Issues in formulating and organising attainment targets in relation to their assessment. In Torrance, H. (ed.) *National Assessment and Testing: A Research Response*. Kendal: British Educational Research Association.

Burke, J. W. (ed.) (1989) *Competency Based Education and Training*. Lewes: Falmer Press.

Burke, J. W. and Jessup, G. (1990) Disentangling validity from reliability. In Horton, J. (ed.) *Assessment Debates*. London: Hodder & Stoughton.

Callender, C. (1992) *Will NVQs Work? Evidence from the Construction Industry*. IMS Report No. 228. University of Sussex: Employment Department/Institute of Manpower Studies.

Chachkin, N. J. (1989) Testing in elementary and secondary schools: can misuse be avoided? In Gifford, B. R. (ed.) *Test Policy and the Politics of Opportunity Allocation: The Workplace and the Law*. Boston: Kluwer.

Choppin, B. and Orr, L. (1976) *Aptitude Testing at 18 +*. Windsor: National Foundation for Educational Research.

Christie, T. and Forrest, G. (1981) *Defining Public Examination Standards*. London: Macmillan.

Clark, L. and Wolf, A. (1991) Assessing the knowledge of Blue Badge Guides. Final Report to the Employment Department. London: Institute of Education.

Collins, R. (1979) *The Credential Society: An Historical Sociology of Education and Stratification*. New York: Academic Press.

Conant, J. B. (1963) *The Education of American Teachers*. New York: McGraw Hill.

Cresswell, M. (1986) Examination grades: how many should there be? *British Educational Research Journal* 12(1): 37–54.

Cresswell, M. (1987) Describing examination performance: grade criteria in public examinations. *Educational Studies*, 13(3): 247–65.

Cronbach, L. (1990) *Essentials of Psychological Testing*. New York: Harper & Row.

Crowley-Bainton, T. and Wolf, A. (1994) *Access to Assessment Initiative*. Sheffield: Employment Department.

Curtain, R. and Hayton, G. (1994) The use and abuse of competency standards in Australia: a comparative perspective. *Assessment in Education*, forthcoming.

Debling, G. (1989) The Employment Department/Training Agency

Standards Programme and NVQs: Implications for education. In Burke, J. W. (ed.) *Competency Based Education and Training*. Lewes: Falmer Press.

Dixon, M. (1993a) Self-imposed stranglehold on recovery. *Financial Times* June 23, p. 14.

Dixon, M. (1993b) Immeasurable waste of human talent. *Financial Times* July 7, p. 11.

Downs, S. (1970) Predicting training potential. *Personnel Management* 2: 26–8.

Dunbar, S. B., Koretz, D. M. and Hoover, H. D. (1991) Quality control in the development and use of performance assessments. *Applied Measurement in Education* 4(4): 289–304.

Edgeworth, F. Y. (1890) The element of chance in competitive examinations. *Proceedings of the Royal Statistical Society*, 461–75 and 644–63.

Eraut, M. and Cole, G. (1993) *Assessing Competence in the Professions*. Technical Report No. 14. Sheffield: Employment Department, Methods Strategy Unit.

Feltham, R. (1988a) Validity of a police assessment centre: a 1–19 year follow-up. *Journal of Occupational Psychology* 61: 129–44.

Feltham, R. (1988b) Assessment centre decision-making: judgmental vs mechanical. *Journal of Occupational Psychology* 61: 237–41.

Fennell, E. (1992) NVQ Implementation Report, Case Study One. *Competence & Assessment* 19: 22–7.

Fennell, E. (1993) NVQ Implementation Report, Case Study Two. *Competence & Assessment* 21: 31–5.

Fletcher, S. (1991) *NVQs Standards and Competence. A Practical Guide for Employers, Managers and Trainers*. London: Kogan Page.

Forrest, G. and Shoesmith, D. J. (1985) *A Second Review of GCE Comparability Studies*. Manchester: Joint Matriculation Board.

Frederiksen, N. (1984) The real test bias: influences of testing on teaching and learning. *American Psychologist* 39: 193–202.

Gardner, K. E. and Williams, A. P. O. (1973) A twenty-five year follow-up of an extended interview selection procedure in the Royal Navy. *Journal of Occupational Psychology* 47: 1–13 and 149–61.

Ghiselli, E. E. (1966) *The validity of occupational aptitude tests*. New York: John Wiley.

Gipps, C. and Wood, R. (1981) The testing of reading in LEAs. The Bullock Report 7 years on. *Educational Studies* 7(2): 133–44.

Girot, E. A. (1993) Assessment of competence in clinical practice – a review of the literature. *Nurse Education Today* 13: 85–90.

Glaser, R. (1963) Instructional technology and the measurement of learning outcomes: some questions. *American Psychologist* 18: 519–21.

Goacher, B. (1984) *Selection Post-16: the role of examination results*. Schools Council Examination Bulletin 45. London: Methuen.

Gonczi, A. (1994) Competency based assessment in the professions in Australia. *Assessment in Education* I.1: 27–45.

Good, F. and Cresswell, M. (1988) *Grading the GCSE*. London: Secondary Examinations Council.

Gordon, M. E. and Cohen S. L. (1973) Training behaviour as a predictor of trainability. *Personnel Psychology* 26: 261–72.

Gordon, M. E. and Kleiman L. S. (1976) The prediction of trainability using a work-sample test and an aptitude test: A direct comparison. *Personnel Psychology* 29: 243–53.

Grant, G., Elbow, P., Ewens, T., Gamson, Z., Kohli, W., Neumann, W., Olesen, V. and Riesman, D. (1979) *On Competence: A Critical Analysis of Competence-based Reforms in Higher Education*. San Francisco: Jossey-Bass.

Habermas, J. (1975) *Legitimation Crisis* (trans. T. McCarthy). Boston: Beacon Press.

Haffenden, I. and Brown, A. (1989) Towards the implementation of competence based curricula in colleges of FE. In Burke, J. W. (ed.) *Competency Based Education and Training*. Lewes: Falmer.

Hambleton, R. K. and Rogers, H. J. (1991) Advances in Criterion-Referenced Measurement. In Hambleton, R. K. and Zaal, J. N. (eds) *Advances in Educational and Psychological Testing*. Boston: Kluwer.

Hambleton, R. K. and Zaal, J. N. (eds) (1991) *Advances in Educational and Psychological Testing*. Boston: Kluwer.

Haney, W. and Madaus, G. F. (1978) Making sense of the competency testing movement. *Harvard Educational Review* 48(4): 464–84.

Harrison, A. (1983) *Profile Reporting of Examination Results*. London: Methuen.

HMSO (1993) *Realising our Potential: A Strategy for Science, Engineering and Technology*. London: HMSO.

Howson, G. (1991) Lessons to be learned. In Howson, G. *National Curricula in Mathematics*. London: The Mathematical Association.

Institute of Education, University of London (1994) Results of a survey of current part time MA students. Internal document: Masters working party.

Jaeger, R. M., Cole, J., Irwin, D. M. and Pratto, D. J. (1980) *An Interactive Structure Judgement Process for Setting Passing Scores on Competency Tests Applied to the North Carolina High School Competency Tests*. University of North Carolina, Greensboro, NC: Centre for Education Research & Evaluation.

Jessup, G. (1991) *Outcomes. NVQs and the Emerging Model of Education and Training*. London: Falmer.

Johnson, C. E. (1974) Competency-based and traditional education practices compared. *Journal of Teacher Education* XXV(4): 355–6.

Kingdon, J., French, S., Pierce, G. and Woodthorpe, A. (1983) Awarding grades on differentiated papers in school examinations at 16 plus. *Educational Research* 25(3): 220–9.

Klimoski, R. and Brickner, M. (1987) Why do assessment centres work? The puzzle of assessment center validity. *Personnel Psychology* 40: 243–60.

Koerner, J. D. (1963) *Miseducation of American Teachers*. New York: Houghton Mifflin.

Koffler, S. L. (1987) Assessing the impact of a State's decision to move from minimum competency testing toward higher level testing for graduation. *Educational Evaluation and Policy Analysis* 9(4): 325–36.

Lazarus, M. (1981) *Goodbye to Excellence: A Critical Look at Minimum Competency Testing*. Washington: NAESP.

Lindquist, E. F. (1951) Preliminary considerations in objective test construction. In Lindquist, E. F. (ed.) *Educational Measurement*, pp. 119–84.

Linn, R. L., Madaus, G. F. and Pedulla, J. J. (1982) Minimum competency testing: cautions on the state of the art. *American Journal of Education* 91: 1–35.

Linn, R. L., Baker, E. L. and Dunbar, S. B. (1991) Complex, performance-based assessment: expectations and validation criteria. *Educational Researcher* 20(8): 15–21.

Little, A. (1984) Education, earnings and productivity – the eternal triangle. In Oxenham, J. (ed.) *Education versus Qualifications?* London: George Allen and Unwin.

Madaus, G. F. (1988) The influence of testing on the curriculum. In Tanner, L. (ed.) *Critical Issues in Curriculum. The 8th Yearbook of the National Society for the Study of Education*. Chicago: University of Chicago Press.

Madaus, G. F. (1991) The effects of important tests on students. *Phi Delta Kappan* November, pp. 226–31.

Madaus, G. F. and Greaney, V. (1985) The Irish experience in competency testing: implications for American education. *American Journal of Education* February, pp. 268–94.

Manpower Services Commission (1981) *A New Training Initiative: Agenda for Action*. London: HMSO.

Manpower Services Commission (1985) *Guidance notes for Two-Year Youth Training Schemes*. Quoted in Wood, R., Johnson, C., Blinkhorn, S., Anderson, S. and Hall, J. (1989) *Boning, Blanching and Backtacking: Assessing performance in the workplace*. R & D Series No. 46. Sheffield: Training Agency.

Manpower Services Commission and Department of Education and

Science (1986) *Review of Vocational Qualifications in England and Wales*. London: HMSO.

Mason, G., Prais, S. J. and Van Ark, B. (1992) *Productivity, Education and Training: Britain and Other Countries Compared*. London: NIESR.

McEvoy, G. M. and Beatty, R. W. (1989) Assessment centers and subordinate appraisals of managers: a seven-year examination of predictive validity. *Personnel Psychology* 42: 37–52.

McGaghie, W. C. (1991) Professional Competence Evaluation. *Educational Researcher* 20(1): 3–9.

McGaghie, W. C. (1993) Evaluating competence for professional practice. In Curry, L. and Wergin, J. F. (eds) *Educating Professionals: Responding to New Expectations for Competence and Accountability*. San Francisco: Jossey Bass.

McHugh, G., Fuller, A. and Lobley, D. (1993) *Why Take NVQs? Perceptions of candidates in the South West*. Lancaster University: Centre for the Study of Education and Training.

Millman, J. (1984) Computer-Based Item Generation. In Berk, R. A. (ed.) *A Guide to Criterion-Referenced Test Construction*. Baltimore: Johns Hopkins University Press.

Mitchell, J. O. (1975) Asssessment center validity: a longitudinal study. *Journal of Applied Psychology* 60(5): 573–9

Mitchell, L. and Wolf, A. (1992) How do you present knowledge in Standards? Paper prepared for Department of Employment Policy Conference, June 1992.

Murnane, R. J. (1991) The case for performance-based licensing. *Phi Delta Kappan* October 137–42.

Murphy, J. (1993) A degree of waste: the economic basis of educational expansion. *Oxford Review of Education* 19(1): 9–32.

Murphy, R. (1982) A further report of investigations into the reliability of marking of GCE examinations. *British Journal of Educational Psychology* 52: 58–63.

NCVQ (1991) *Guide to National Vocational Qualifications*. London: NCVQ.

Newman, J. H. (1852: reprinted 1928) *Selected Discourses on Liberal Knowledge*. Dublin: James Duffy.

Norcini, J. J. and Shea, J. A. (1993) Increasing pressures for recertification and relicensure. In Curry, L. and Wergin, J. F. (eds) *Educating Professionals: Responding to New Expectations for Competence and Accountability*. San Francisco: Jossey Bass.

Norris, N. (1991) The trouble with competence. *Cambridge Journal of Education* 21(3): 331–41.

Noss, R., Goldstein, H. and Hoyles, C. (1989) Graded assessment and learning hierarchies in mathematics. *British Educational Research Journal* 15(2): 109–20.

Nuttall, D. L. (1987) The validity of assessments. *European Journal of Psychology of Education* 2: 109–18.

Orr, L. and Nuttall, D. (1983) *Determining Standards in the Proposed Single System of Examining at 16+*. London: Schools Council.

Penington, D. G. (1992) What Do We Mean By Tertiary Education? The University Perspective. Paper presented to a national conference on *What do we mean by Tertiary Education?*, Melbourne, Australia, 16 December.

Pollard, A., Broadfoot, P., Goll, P., Osborn, M. and Abbott, D. (1994) *Changing English Primary Schools? The Impact of the Educational Reform Act at Key Stage One*. London: Cassell.

Pollitt, A., Hutchinson, C., Entwistle, N. and DeLuca, C. (1985) *What Makes Exam Questions Difficult?* Edinburgh: Scottish Academic Press.

Popham, W. J. (1978) *Criterion-Referenced Measurement*. Englewood Cliffs NJ: Prentice-Hall.

Popham, W. J. (1984) Specifying the domain of content or behaviours. In Berk, R.A. (ed.) *A Guide to Criterion-Referenced Test Construction*. Baltimore: Johns Hopkins University Press.

Prais, S. (1989) How Europe would see the new British initiative for standardising vocational qualifications. *National Institute Economic Review* 129: 52–4.

Prais, S. (1991) Vocational qualifications in Britain and Europe: Theory and Practice. *National Institute Economic Review* 136: 86–92.

Prais, S. (1993) 'Economic Performance and Education: The Nature of Britain's Deficiencies'. Keynes Lecture on Economics. London: The British Academy.

Priestley, M. (1982) *Performance Assessment in Education and Training: Alternative Techniques*. Englewood Cliffs NJ: Educational Technology Publications.

Raffe, D. (1991) Paper prepared for US Department of Education/OECD Seminar. *Linkages in Vocational-Technical Education and Training*, Phoenix, Arizona.

Riesman, D. (1979) Society's demands for competence. In Grant, G., Elbow, P., Ewens, T., Gamson, Z., Kohli, W., Neumann, W., Olesen, V. and Reisman, D. *On Competence: A Critical Analysis of Competence-Based Reforms in Higher Education*. San Francisco: Jossey-Bass.

Robertson, I. and Downs, S. (1979) Learning and the prediction of performance: development of trainability testing in the United Kingdom. *Journal of Applied Psychology* 64(1): 42–50.

Robertson, I. T. and Kandola, R. S. (1982) Work sample tests:

validity, adverse impact and applicant reaction. *Journal of Occupational Psychology* 55: 171–83.

Roe, R. and Grueter, M. (1991) Developments in Personnel Selection Methodology. In Hambleton and Zaal (eds) *Advances in Educational and Psychological Testing*. Boston: Kluwer.

Rose, R. and Wignanek, G. (1991) *Training Without Trainers? How Germany avoids Britain's supply-side bottleneck*. London: Anglo-German Foundation.

Samson, G. E., Graue, M. E., Weinstein, T. and Walberg, H. J. (1984) Academic and occupational performance: a quantitative synthesis. *American Educational Research Journal* 21(2): 311–21.

Scottish Office Education Department (1991) *National Tests 1991: Report of Moderation*. Edinburgh: Scottish Office.

Shackleton, J. R. (1992) *Training Too Much? A sceptical look at the economics of skill provision in the UK*. Hobart Paper 118. London: Institute of Economic Affairs.

Shepard, L. A. and Kreitzer, A. E. (1987) The Texas teacher test. *Educational Researcher* Aug/Sept., 22–31.

Smith, F. D. (1991) Work samples as measures of performance. In Wigdor, A. and Green, B. *Performance Assessment for the Workplace*. Washington DC: National Academy Press.

Smith, M. L. and Shepard, L. (1988) Kindergarten readiness and retention. A qualitative study of teachers' beliefs and practices. *American Educational Research Journal* 25(3): 307–33.

Smithers, A. (1993) 'All Our Futures: Britain's Education Revolution'. *Dispatches Report on Education* London: Channel Four Television.

Smithers, A. and Robinson, P. (1989) *Increasing Participation in Higher Education*. London: BP Educational Services.

Steedman, H. and Hawkins, J. (1994) Shifting foundations: the impact of NVQs on youth training in the building trades. *National Institute Economic Review*, 149, 93–101.

Stobart, G. (1991) GCSE meets Key Stage 4: something had to give. *Cambridge Journal of Education* 21(2): 177–88.

Torrance, H. (ed.) (1994) *Evaluating Authentic Assessment*. Buckingham: Open University Press.

Training Agency (1988/9) *Development of Assessable Standards for National Certification. Guidance Notes 1–8*. Sheffield: Training Agency.

Tuxworth, E. (1989) Competence based education and training: background and origins. In Burke, J. W. (ed.) *Competency Based Education and Training*. Lewes: Falmer Press.

US Departments of Education and Labor (1993) *Preamble to Goals 2000: Educate America Act*. Washington DC: US Departments of Education and Labor.

Vickerstaff, S. (1991) The training needs of small firms. *Human Resource Management Journal* 2(3): 2–15.

Watson, J. and Wolf, A. (1991) Return to Sender. *Times Educational Supplement* September 6.

Weber, M. (1964) *The Theory of Social and Economic Organization* (trans. A. M. Henderson and Talcott Parsons). New York: The Free Press.

Wernimont, P. F. and Campbell, J. P. (1968) Signs, samples and criteria. *Journal of Applied Psychology* 52: 372–76.

Wigdor, A. and Green, B. (1991) *Performance Assessment for the Workplace*. Washington DC: National Academy Press.

Williams, I. C. and Boreham, N. C. (1971) *The Predictive Value of CSE Grades in Further Education (Schools Council Examination Bulletin 24)*. London: Evans/Methuen Educational.

Wingrove, J., Jones, A. and Herot, P. (1985) The predictive validity of pre- and post-discussion assessment centre ratings. *Journal of Occupational Psychology* 58, 189–92.

Winter, S. S. (1982) The adoption of competency-based regulations for teacher certification in Massachusetts. *Compare* 12(2): 153–65.

Wolf, A. (1990) Testing investigations. In Dowling, P. and Noss, R. (eds) *Mathematics versus the National Curriculum*. London: Falmer.

Wolf, A. (1993a) *Assessment Issues and Problems in a Criterion-based System* London: Further Education Unit.

Wolf, A. (1993b) Some final thoughts: vocational education policy in a European context. *European Journal of Education* (28): 2.

Wolf, A. (1994) Authentic assessments in a competitive sector: institutional prerequisites and cautionary tales. In Torrance, H. (ed.) *Evaluating Authentic Assessment*. Buckingham: Open University Press.

Wolf, A. and Silver, R. (1986) *Work-Based Learning: Trainee Assessment by Supervisors*. Sheffield: MSC R & D Series No. 33.

Wolf, A. and Silver, R. (1990) 'Measuring broad skills. The prediction of skills transfer and retention over time. A review of the literature.' Paper prepared for the Employment Department. London: Institute of Education.

Wolf, A., Silver, R., Collins, P. and Tambini, D. (1994) *Assessing Broad Skills. Final Report to the Employment Department*. London: Institute of Education.

Wood, R. (1985) *Assessing achievements to standards*. Report to the Manpower Services Commission.

Wood, R. (1991) *Assessment and Testing: A survey of research*. Cambridge: Cambridge University Press.

Wood, R., Johnson, C., Blinkhorn, S., Anderson, S. and Hall, J. (1989) *Boning, Blanching and Backtacking: Assessing performance in the workplace*. R & D Series No. 46. Sheffield: Training Agency.

INDEX

HOW TO GET A PhD (2nd edition)
A HANDBOOK FOR STUDENTS AND THEIR SUPERVISORS
Estelle M. Phillips and D. S. Pugh

This is a handbook and survival manual for PhD students, providing a practical, realistic understanding of the processes of doing research for a doctorate. It discusses many important issues often left unconsidered, such as the importance of time management and how to achieve it, and how to overcome the difficulties of communicating with supervisors. Consideration is given to the particular problems of groups such as women, part-time and overseas students.

The book also provides practical insights for supervisors, focusing on how to monitor and, if necessary, improve supervisory practice. It assists senior academic administrators by examining the responsibilities that universities have for providing an adequate service for research students. This is a revised and updated second edition; it will be as warmly welcomed as the first edition:

> One way of providing a more supportive environment for PhD students is for supervisors to recommend this book.
>
> *(Teaching News)*

> Warmly recommended as a bedside companion, both to those hoping to get a PhD and to those who have the responsibility of guiding them, often with very little support themselves.
>
> *(Higher Education Review)*

> This is an excellent book. Its style is racy and clear . . . an impressive array of information, useful advice and comment gleaned from the authors' systematic study and experience over many years . . . should be required reading not only for those contemplating doctoral study but also for all supervisors, new and experienced.
>
> *(Higher Education)*

Contents

224pp   0 335 19214 9 (Paperback)

THE HUMAN NATURE OF LEARNING
SELECTIONS FROM THE WORK OF M. L. J. ABERCROMBIE

Jennifer Nias (ed.)

For over forty years M. L. J. Abercrombie contributed through her teaching, research, lecturing and writing, to the theory and practice of education. In particular, she carried out pioneer research into the use of groups in learning with medical, architectural and education students, and she shared with diverse audiences in many countries her extensive knowledge and expertise as a teacher who used the methods and principles of group analytic psychotherapy. Her best known publication, *The Anatomy of Judgement* was reissued in 1989 (Free Association Books). Many of her other writings are now difficult to locate because she was a prolific writer whose work is scattered through a host of journals, conference proceedings and books.

This book brings together for the first time an edited selection from the educational writings of Jane Abercrombie. The extracts are arranged in four parts. The first gives an overview of her educational convictions, of the development of her research and thinking. The second illustrates the way in which, throughout her work, three themes – the selective and projective nature of perception and reasoning; the difficulty that human beings experience in changing; the subtlety and complexity of communication – continually interact with and enrich one another. The third part focuses in greater detail upon group analysis, its relevance to and use in higher education. The fourth gives detailed examples of 'free' or 'associative' group discussion as she used it in her own work with students. *The Human Nature of Learning* will be of interest to teachers in higher education; to group conductors; and to students and teachers in all occupations in which the ability to communicate sensitively and productively with others is of central importance.

Contents
Introduction – Overview: a personal account of research into higher education – Perceiving, changing and communicating – 'Associative' group discussion in higher education – Teaching in groups: examples of practice – Bibliography – Index.

192pp   0 335 09333 7 (Paperback)   0 335 09334 5 (Hardback)

DOING YOUR RESEARCH PROJECT (2nd edition)
A GUIDE FOR FIRST-TIME RESEARCHERS IN EDUCATION AND
SOCIAL SCIENCE

Judith Bell

If you are a beginner researcher, the problems facing you are much the
same whether you are producing a small project, an MEd dissertation
or a PhD thesis. You will need to select a topic; identify the objectives of
your study; plan and design a suitable methodology; devise research
instruments; negotiate access to institutions, material and people; collect,
analyse and present information; and finally, produce a well-written report
or dissertation. Whatever the scale of the undertaking, you will have to
master techniques and devise a plan of action which does not attempt more
than the limitations of expertise, time and access permit.

We all learn to do research by actually doing it, but a great deal of time
can be wasted and goodwill dissipated by inadequate preparation. This
book aims to provide you with the tools to do the job, to help you avoid
some of the pitfalls and time-wasting false trails that can eat into your time,
to establish good research habits, and to take you from the stage of choos-
ing a topic through to the production of a well-planned, methodologically
sound and well-written final report or dissertation on time.

Doing Your Research Project serves as a source of reference and guide to
good practice for all beginner researchers, whether undergraduate and
postgraduate students or professionals such as teachers or social workers
undertaking investigations in Education and the Social Sciences. This
second edition retains the basic structure of the very successful first edition
whilst incorporating some important new material.

Contents
*Introduction – Approaches to educational research – Planning the project –
Keeping records and making notes – Reviewing the literature – Negotiating
access and the problems of inside research – The analysis of documentary
evidence – Designing and administering questionnaires – Planning and
conducting interviews – Diaries – Observation studies – Interpretation
and presentation of the evidence – Postscript – References – Index.*

192pp   0 335 19094 4 (Paperback)